EX LIBRIS

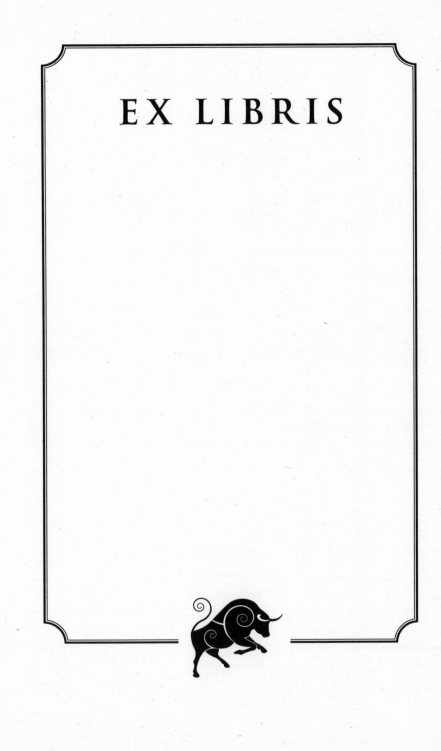

Also by Marc Morris

The Norman Conquest

A Great and Terrible King:
Edward I and the Forging of Britain

The Bigod Earls of Norfolk in the Thirteenth Century

Castle: A History of the Buildings that
Shaped Medieval Britain

MARC MORRIS

KING JOHN

Treachery, Tyranny and the
Road to Magna Carta

HUTCHINSON
LONDON

3 5 7 9 10 8 6 4 2 1

Hutchinson
20 Vauxhall Bridge Road
London SW1V 2SA

Hutchinson is part of the Penguin Random House group of companies whose
addresses can be found at global.penguinrandomhouse.com.

First published by Hutchinson in 2015

www.randomhouse.co.uk

A CIP catalogue record for this book is available from the British Library.

ISBN 9780091954239

Typeset by Palimpsest Book Production Ltd, Falkirk, Stirlingshire

Printed and bound by Clays Ltd, St Ives plc

Penguin Random House is committed to a sustainable future for our business,
our readers and our planet. This book is made from Forest Stewardship
Council® certified paper.

To William
my treasure

Contents

Acknowledgements

My thanks as usual to all the experts who have taken the time to respond to my inquiries: Adrian Ailes, Nick Barratt, Paul Brand, David Carpenter, David Crouch, Rick Heiser, John Maddicott, David Morrison, Nigel Saul, Brendan Smith, Matthew Strickland, Paul Webster and Louise Wilkinson. I would especially like to acknowledge the kindness of Harriet Webster and her publisher at Boydell, Richard Barber, for allowing me to make use of her translations of Ralph of Coggeshall's chronicle and the Dunstable Annals ahead of publication. Thanks also to Nick Vincent for sending me transcripts of John's charters that have been collected and edited as part of the Angevin Acta project, and to Colin Veach for letting me have an advance copy of his excellent article on William de Briouze. I've enjoyed discussing King John on many occasions with Sophie Ambler, who lent me books and articles that would otherwise have been hard to obtain, and kept me informed of all the exciting research being carried out by the rest of the team at the Magna Carta Project. Once again I am enormously grateful to John Gillingham for reading the whole book in draft and informing me of its errors. Any that remain are all my own fault. At LAW I am indebted as ever to my agent, Julian Alexander, and his assistant, Ben Clark. The team at Hutchinson

– Sarah Rigby, Jocasta Hamilton, Stephanie Sweeney, Laura Deacon, and Najma Finlay – have been supportive and enthusiastic about this book from the first, and ensured that it was ready in time for the 800th anniversary of Magna Carta. My thanks to David Milner for his skilful copy-editing, Mary Chamberlain for her careful proof-reading, Jeff Edwards for drawing the maps and family tree, Charlotte Lippmann for her picture research and Alex Bell for compiling the index. Lastly, thanks and love to Cie, Peter and William for their support and patience, especially during the final months of writing. I look forward to spending more time with them now it is all done.

A Note on Money

In John's day (and indeed until the currency was decimalized in 1971), money in England was measured in pounds, shillings and pence: twelve pennies made a shilling, and twenty shillings made a pound. The only type of coin in circulation was the silver penny, so a pound was a weighty bag of 240 coins. The average income for a baron was about £200 per annum, and even a man who took home £20 a year would have been considered quite well-off. Money was also counted in marks, which were equivalent to 160 pennies, or two-thirds of a pound.

People being tortured during the reign of King John. A drawing
by the thirteenth-century chronicler Matthew Paris.

List of Illustrations

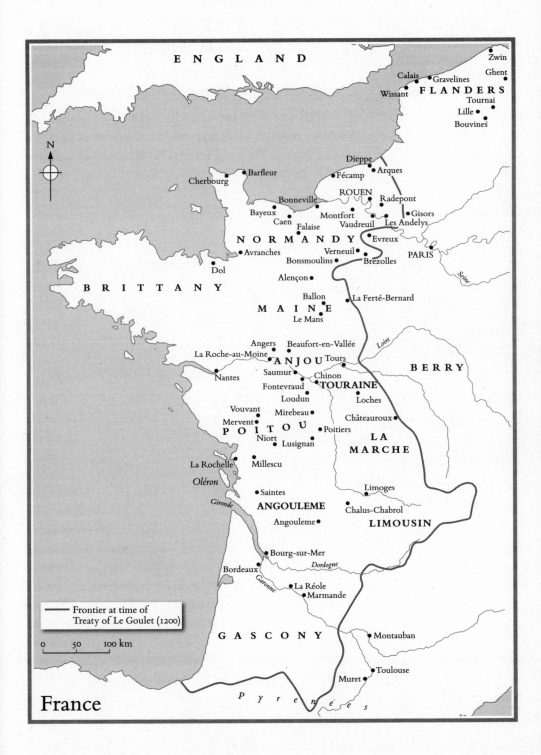

ENGLAND

Zwin
Calais Ghent
Gravelines
Wissant FLANDERS
Tournai
Lille
Bouvines

Dieppe
Arques
Cherbourg Barfleur Fécamp
Bonneville ROUEN Radepont
Bayeux Montfort Gisors
Caen Vaudreuil Les Andelys
Falaise
NORMANDY Evreux
Avranches Verneuil
Bonsmoulins Brézolles PARIS
Dol Alençon
Seine

BRITTANY
Ballon La Ferté-Bernard
MAINE
Le Mans

Loire
Angers Beaufort-en-Vallée
La Roche-au-Moine Tours BERRY
ANJOU
Nantes Saumur Chinon
Fontevraud TOURAINE
Loudun Loches
Vouvant Mirebeau
Mervent Châteauroux
POITOU Poitiers
Niort LA
Lusignan MARCHE
La Rochelle
Millescu
Oléron Saintes
Limoges
Gironde ANGOULEME Chalus-Chabrol
Angouleme LIMOUSIN

Bourg-sur-Mer
Bordeaux Dordogne
Garonne La Réole
Marmande

Frontier at time of
Treaty of Le Goulet (1200)

0   50   100 km

GASCONY Montauban

Toulouse
Muret

Pyrenees

France

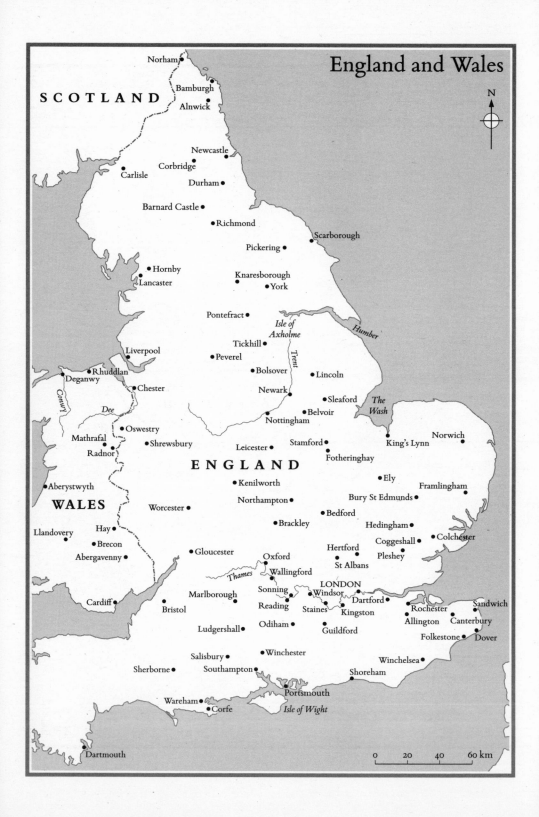

England and Wales

N

SCOTLAND

Norham
Bamburgh
Alnwick
Newcastle
Corbridge
Carlisle
Durham
Barnard Castle
Richmond
Scarborough
Pickering
Hornby
Knaresborough
Lancaster
York
Pontefract
Isle of Axholme
Tickhill
Liverpool
Peverel
Trent
Rhuddlan
Bolsover
Deganwy
Lincoln
Chester
Newark
Dee
Sleaford
The Wash
Belvoir
Oswestry
Nottingham
Mathrafal
Shrewsbury
Stamford
King's Lynn
Norwich
Radnor
Leicester
Fotheringhay
ENGLAND
Aberystwyth
Kenilworth
Ely
Framlingham
Bury St Edmunds
WALES
Northampton
Worcester
Bedford
Hedingham
Coggeshall
Colchester
Hay
Brackley
Hertford
Pleshey
Llandovery
Brecon
St Albans
Abergavenny
Gloucester
Oxford
Thames
Wallingford
LONDON
Cardiff
Marlborough
Sonning
Windsor
Dartford
Rochester
Sandwich
Bristol
Reading
Staines
Kingston
Allington
Canterbury
Ludgershall
Odiham
Guildford
Folkestone
Dover
Salisbury
Winchester
Sherborne
Southampton
Winchelsea
Shoreham
Wareham
Corfe
Portsmouth
Isle of Wight
Dartmouth

Humber

Conwy

0   20   40   60 km

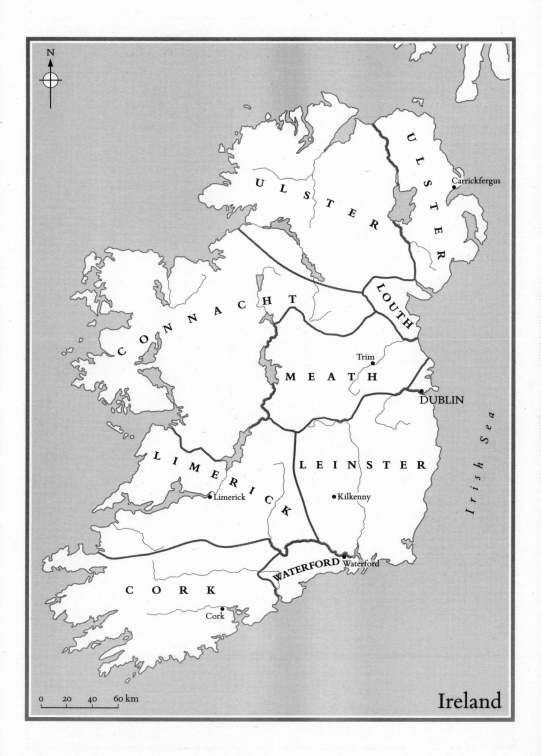

N

ULSTER

ULSTER

Carrickfergus

CONNACHT

LOUTH

MEATH

Trim

DUBLIN

LIMERICK

LEINSTER

Limerick

Kilkenny

Irish Sea

WATERFORD

Waterford

CORK

Cork

0   20   40   60 km

Ireland

Family Tree of King John

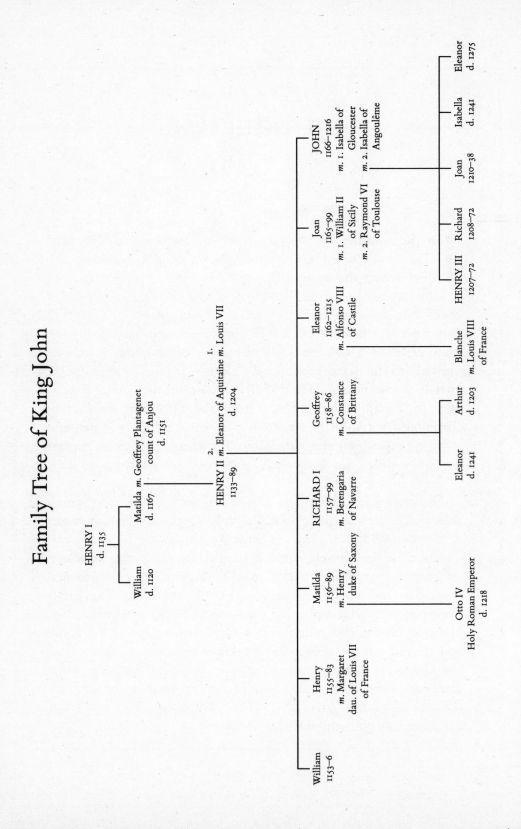

HENRY I
d. 1135

William
d. 1120

Matilda *m.* Geoffrey Plantagenet
d. 1167   count of Anjou
             d. 1151

1.
2. HENRY II *m.* Eleanor of Aquitaine *m.* Louis VII
   1133–89   d. 1204

William
1153–6

Henry
1155–83
m. Margaret
dau. of Louis VII
of France

Matilda
1156–89
m. Henry
duke of Saxony

RICHARD I
1157–99
m. Berengaria
of Navarre

Geoffrey
1158–86
m. Constance
of Brittany

Eleanor
1162–1215
m. Alfonso VIII
of Castile

Joan
1165–99
m. 1. William II
of Sicily
m. 2. Raymond VI
of Toulouse

JOHN
1166–1216
m. 1. Isabella of
Gloucester
m. 2. Isabella of
Angoulême

Otto IV
Holy Roman Emperor
d. 1218

Eleanor
d. 1241

Arthur
d. 1203

Blanche
m. Louis VIII
of France

HENRY III
1207–72

Richard
1208–72

Joan
1210–38

Isabella
d. 1241

Eleanor
d. 1275

Introduction

In the summer of 1797 a group of workmen in Worcester Cathedral caused a sensation, locally if not nationally, by discovering the body of King John.

John's tomb had long stood in the middle of the cathedral's choir, but the consensus view in 1797 was that it was empty. Although the stone likeness (or effigy) on top dated from not long after the king's death in 1216, the tomb chest had been created in the sixteenth century in the style of more recent burials (most notably Henry VIII's older brother, Arthur, who died in 1502). It was known from the testimony of ancient chronicles that John had been buried in the Lady Chapel, and so it was assumed that, although his effigy had been moved in Tudor times, his bones had been left undisturbed in their original resting place.

The cathedral clergy found John's tomb a cause of 'much annoyance', because its central position obstructed the approach to the altar, and their plan was to move it to some more convenient part of the church. And so, on 17 July 1797, the workmen set about dismantling it. They removed the effigy and the cracked stone slab underneath, to discover that the chest had been partitioned by two brick walls, and the sections in between filled with builders' rubble. But when they removed the sides of the tomb and cleared out the debris, the workmen, 'to their astonishment', found a stone coffin. Immediately the dean and chapter of the cathedral were convened, as well as some local worthies with relevant expertise (the antiquarian Mr James Ross, and Mr Sandford, 'an eminent surgeon of Worcester').

Inside the coffin they found 'the entire remains of King John'. His corpse had obviously decomposed somewhat in the course of nearly six centuries. Despite being embalmed, some parts had putrefied, and so 'a vast quantity of the dry skins of maggots were dispersed over the body'. Parts of the body had also been displaced, presumably when it was moved in the sixteenth century. A section of the left arm was found lying at an angle on the chest; the upper jaw was found near the elbow. But otherwise the king was arranged in exactly the same position as his effigy, and was similarly attired. He was dressed from head to foot in a robe of crimson damask (a rich fabric of wool woven with silk) and in his left hand – as on the effigy – he held a sword, in a scabbard, both badly decayed. Curiously, however, whereas on the effigy John wore a crown, his skull was wearing a coif, which the antiquarians took to be a monk's cowl, placed on the king's head after his death to help reduce his time in Purgatory. Measuring the body they found that John had been five foot six-and-a-half inches tall.

The experts might have continued their investigations further, but were prevented from doing so by a large number of people who had crowded into the cathedral to see the dead monarch. 'It is much to be regretted', explained the antiquarian Valentine Green in his published account of the exhumation, 'that the impatience of the multitude to view the royal remains, so unexpectedly found, should have become so ungovernable, as to make it necessary to close up the object of their curiosity.' He was not exaggerating. In the short time that the tomb was open, several bits of John's body were removed by souvenir hunters. His thumb bone was later recovered and can now be seen in the cathedral's own archives, along with some fragments of sandals and stocking, obtained at auction by Edward Elgar. Two of the king's teeth, stolen by a stationer's apprentice in 1797, were 'secretly treasured' until 1923, when they were handed over to the Worcester County Museum.[1]

★ ★ ★

It is easy to understand the excitement of the people of Worcester in 1797. King John is one of those characters from English history who has always exerted a hold on the public's imagination. Almost everyone, even if they know nothing else about the Middle Ages, must feel they know something about him. Unlike other famous medieval monarchs, this is not down to Shakespeare, whose *Life and Times of King John* is one of his worst (and hence least-performed) plays. We are introduced to John much earlier, as children, through the tales of Robin Hood. My own introduction to him, I'm sure, was Disney's *Robin Hood*, released in 1973 (the year I was born), in which the king, voiced by Peter Ustinov, is memorably portrayed by a scrawny lion, with a head too small for the crown he has pinched from his older brother, Richard the Lionheart.

As we will see, there is an element of truth in this story – John did at one point try to usurp the throne from Richard. But the association of John with Robin Hood is pure fiction. The tales of Robin Hood were not written down until the fifteenth century, and in their earliest versions they are said to take place during the time of 'King Edward'. It was not until the sixteenth century that a Scottish writer, John Mair, thought to relocate them to the reign of Richard the Lionheart. From that point, however, the association of John and Robin took firm root. The story was given an immense boost by Walter Scott in his 1820 novel, *Ivanhoe*, which became the basis for the celebrated 1938 Errol Flynn film, *The Adventures of Robin Hood*, itself the basis of the Disney animation.[2]

To get to the real King John, we have to look at the evidence from his own day – what was said about him by contemporary chroniclers, and what can be learned about him from official records. John's reign was a watershed moment in many important respects, including the amount of government archive. From the time of his accession in 1199, the king's chancery, or writing office, began to keep copies of the documents it produced by enrolling them, and these rolls have for the most part survived. (They are now housed in the National Archives at Kew.) As a result we have far more letters, charters, memoranda – in short, far more information – about John than we do for any of his predecessors. Most of the time we can see where he is, who he is with, and what is on his agenda.

Once he is king, that is. One of the problems with telling John's story is that he was the youngest of five brothers, and as such did not grow up expecting to inherit very much at all, let alone the most extensive dominion in Europe. There *is* evidence for John before his accession, but it is altogether more patchy. His life prior to that point has moments of high drama, but there are also long periods during which he almost completely disappears. For this reason, I decided to start my account a few years into his reign, and to look back to the earlier episodes in his life. Plotting the book in this way, it seemed to fall quite naturally into two themes or strands, with a turning point in 1203.

That, therefore, is where we find John at the beginning of Chapter One.

1

Under Attack

1203

In 1203 King John was the ruler of a vast international empire. Besides being king of England he was master of much of south Wales and lord of Ireland. He was also duke of Normandy, count of Anjou and duke of Aquitaine, meaning that he ruled all of what we would now regard as western France, from the English Channel to the Pyrenees. From north to south his authority extended 1,000 miles, and half that distance from east to west. Travellers could pass from the border of Scotland to the border of Spain without ever leaving his territories. Millions of people, speaking at least half a dozen different languages, were his subjects. By any measure, his was the most important and powerful dominion in Europe.[1]

But in the spring of 1203 it was a dominion under attack. John had a rival in the shape of the king of France, Philip II – or Philip Augustus, as he had been dubbed by an admiring contemporary chronicler. At thirty-seven Philip was just one year older than John, but he had been a king for much longer – twenty-three years to John's four. The kingdom he ruled was much smaller than the France of today, but since the start of his reign Philip had been consolidating and extending his power. He had, for example, completely transformed his capital at Paris, giving it new walls, paved streets and a palatial royal castle called the Louvre, expanding the city so that it was many times larger than it had been before. He had long nurtured similar plans to expand the size of his kingdom, and in 1203 he put them into action.[2]

Philip began his assault on John's empire a week after Easter, sailing down the River Loire into the heart of Anjou and seizing the castle at Saumur. At the same moment his allies in the region – John's rebellious subjects – successfully besieged several other castles and occupied the city of Le Mans. In this way John's enemies cut his empire in two, separating Normandy from the provinces further south. Normandy was Philip's main target, and he immediately moved his forces against it, quickly taking a string of major fortresses along its eastern frontier, some of which surrendered to him without a struggle.[3]

John himself was in Normandy at this time, moving between the castles on the frontier and the duchy's principal city, Rouen. According to one chronicler, messengers came to him with news of the invasion, saying 'the king of France has entered your lands as an enemy, has taken such-and-such castles, carried off their keepers ignominiously bound to their horses' tails, and disposes of your property at will, without anyone resisting him'. John's reaction, however, was reportedly one of blithe indifference. 'Let him do so,' he replied. 'Whatever he now seizes I will one day recover.'[4]

This is almost certainly inaccurate and unfair. The chronicler who reports these words, Roger of Wendover, was one of the king's harshest critics. He was a contemporary, in that he lived through John's reign, but he did not write his chronicle until after the reign was over. His account is extremely valuable, sometimes providing credible information that cannot be found elsewhere. But it also contains stories that are demonstrably false, and is shot through with hindsight and moral judgement. Describing John's behaviour at the time of Philip's attack, for instance, Wendover accuses him of 'incorrigible idleness', claiming that he feasted sumptuously every day and enjoyed a long lie-in every morning.[5]

In fact we can see from John's itinerary that during these weeks he was constantly on the move, and other sources state that his first reaction was to try to negotiate, offering the French king any sum of money to break off his attack. When this failed, he pinned his hopes on the intervention of the pope, who wrote to Philip in May, exhorting him to desist or face the Church's condemnation.[6] Then, in the middle of July, John tried to seize the military initiative. He succeeded in recovering a castle in central Normandy, Montfort-sur-Risle, whose lord had defected at the start of the crisis, and the following month he came close to retaking two other castles, Alençon and Brezolles, on the duchy's southern border, but in both cases he retreated on being told that a French army was approaching. Philip meanwhile convened a council of his own bishops and barons who collectively told the pope to mind his own business. Towards the end of August he resumed his offensive, marching his army down the River Seine to begin his assault on the greatest of all John's defences.[7]

Today Château Gaillard is a badly scarred ruin, set high on a rock above a bend in the Seine, about twenty miles south-east of Rouen. In 1203 it was a brand-new building, with pristine stone-work and regal interiors, the most technologically up-to-date fortress in Europe. It had been constructed just a few years earlier by John's older brother, and immediate predecessor, Richard the Lionheart. Richard had waged a long and inconclusive war against Philip Augustus along the Norman–French border, and Château Gaillard – literally, 'the Saucy Castle' – had been created as both a defence for Rouen and a forward base for future conquests. It was built at lightning speed between 1196 and 1198, and at the gargantuan cost of £12,000. (The mighty Dover Castle, built a decade earlier, had cost only half as much.) Richard's new fortress was nonetheless perfectly realized and, in his own immodest opinion, invincible. According to one contemporary, the king had boasted that he could hold it even if its walls were made out of butter.[8]

Philip was finally ready to put the Lionheart's bold claim to the test. Before he could assault Château Gaillard itself, however,

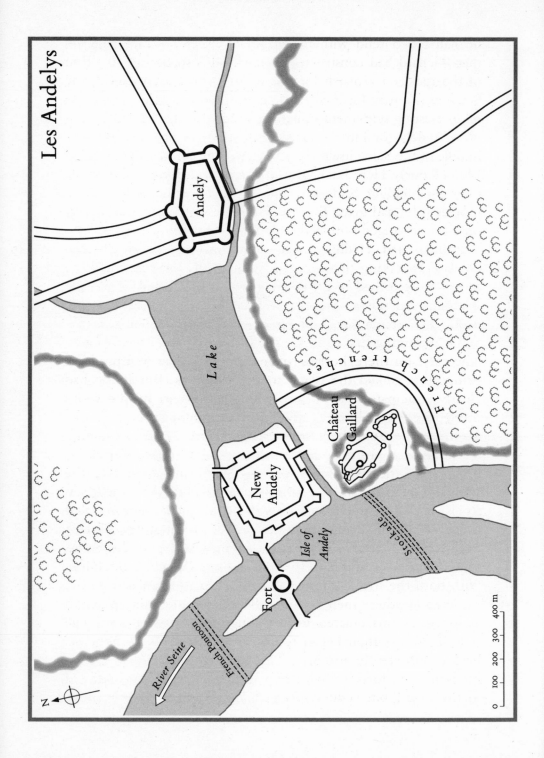

Les Andelys

Andely

Lake

New Andely

Château Gaillard

French trenches

Isle of Andely

Stockade

Fort

French pontoon

River Seine

N

0 100 200 300 400 m

he had to contend with the elaborate series of outer defences that Richard had constructed in the castle's shadow. At the foot of the rock, on a marsh formed by two small tributaries of the Seine, was a new fortified town. It was about a mile to the west of an existing settlement called Andely, and so became known as New Andely (or Little Andely). Opposite this new town, in the middle of the Seine itself, was a long, narrow island – the so-called Isle of Andely. Here Richard had created a crossing of the whole river by building bridges to the shore on either side, and to protect it he had given the island a fortress of its own: an octagonal tower, ringed with a double set of wooden palisades.[9]

Philip's first challenge was therefore to isolate Château Gaillard by taking these outer defences. The way in which he did so is described in great detail by his chaplain, William the Breton, who was an eyewitness.[10] Seeking to avoid the castle itself, the French king led his army up the left bank of the Seine, intending first to tackle the fortress on the Isle of Andely. The garrison there, hearing of his approach, had destroyed the bridge that linked the island to the left bank. But Philip had clearly anticipated such a move, for on their arrival his troops immediately set about creating a replacement crossing, requisitioning boats and barges to transport the necessary building materials into position. This itself was a perilous undertaking, because a little upstream from the island, directly under the walls of Château Gaillard, King Richard had planted a wooden stockade across the river, prohibiting all traffic beyond that point. To get his bridge-building supplies through this barrier, Philip had to send a team of swimmers out into the Seine, armed with axes, and have them hack out a breach. Contending with both the strong current and a shower of missiles from the castle above, these men sustained heavy casualties, but at length an opening was created wide enough for boats to pass. The rest of Philip's men began to construct an elaborate pontoon bridge, sufficiently strong and massive to bear the weight of his army, and fortified with two large towers. It was built not to the island, but right across the Seine to the opposite shore.

As soon as it was completed, the king led the bulk of his forces across to form a new camp on the river's eastern bank, directly menacing the new town of Andely, and leaving the garrison of the island cut off from both sides.

News of the attack on Andely had by now reached the ears of King John, who responded by returning to Rouen and devising a plan for the island's relief. Two separate forces would mount a daring night-time assault. The first, consisting of knights and mercenaries, would proceed along the left bank of the Seine and tackle the French soldiers who remained on that side of the river. The second would be a maritime force: a fleet of galleys, built by Richard to patrol and defend the Seine, together with other ships captained by pirates, would smash through the French pontoon, bringing supplies to the besieged garrison on the island.

The plan was put into immediate effect. The land army was not led by John, who remained in Rouen, but by William Marshal (or 'the Marshal', as contemporaries called him), a military veteran in his mid-fifties, who had plenty of experience executing such devious operations. Advancing along the left bank as agreed, his army fell upon the sleeping French camp in the pre-dawn darkness. Since most of those sleeping there were apparently merchants and other hangers-on rather than soldiers, it was an easy victory, with over 200 said to have been killed. Others tried to escape across the pontoon bridge in such numbers that it broke under the strain. The fleet, it seemed, would have no difficulty in completing the bridge's destruction.

Except that the fleet was nowhere to be seen. While the Marshal and his men had made their way along the river unopposed, the naval force had run into unexpected difficulties – John's scheme had failed to take into account the strength of the tide his oarsmen would have to contend with. In the meantime, the French who were camped on the opposite side of the river had been woken by the noise of the assault and the panicked arrival of their fugitive countrymen. Under the direction of William des Barres, a commander with no less experience than William Marshal, the rout was arrested. Hasty repairs were carried out to the bridge by torchlight, and, as soon as it was passable, des Barres led the French back across to confront their enemies. Surprised at this unexpected reversal, the Marshal's men were now defeated in their turn, with many killed or taken prisoner. The Marshal himself escaped.

The French, thinking the assault was over, recrossed the river, either to celebrate their victory or return to their beds. But a short while later the cry to arms again rang out around their camp: the mercenary fleet had been sighted. The fleet, if not quite so large as William the Breton would have us believe, was clearly a formidable fighting force; there can be little doubt that, had it arrived as planned – in tandem with the Marshal's army and under cover of darkness – the French lines would have been broken and the Isle of Andely resupplied. But, delayed as they were, the naval forces were deprived of the element of surprise, for by this point the sun was rising. By the time they reached the pontoon bridge, both banks of the river and the bridge itself were lined with French soldiers, and the ships sailed into a blizzard of arrows, stones and crossbow bolts. Some of them did crash into the pontoon, and their crews began desperately hacking at its timbers and cables. But the defenders engaged them in savage hand-to-hand combat, and the river ran red with blood. When two of the ships at the front of the fleet were sunk by a giant falling timber, the remainder retreated in confusion, back in the direction of Rouen. Two more ships were captured by the French as they fled.

Having beaten off their assailants, the French made an immediate attempt to take the island. According to William the Breton, this was achieved by a heroic individual who swam out to an undefended spot on its eastern side and threw firebombs at the wooden palisades surrounding the fortress. Very quickly the whole complex was engulfed in flames. Those members of the garrison who had taken refuge in the cellars of the tower perished; those who escaped were forced to surrender to their attackers. Seeing that the island had fallen, the citizens of New Andely abandoned the town and fled up the hill to seek refuge in Château Gaillard.

Philip occupied the deserted town and settled down to besiege his main target.

With the French in total control of both the Seine and the surrounding countryside, there was no question of attempting another relief operation. Instead John tried to lure Philip away by launching an assault on his allies. In early September he left Rouen with the remainder of his forces, heading in the direction of Brittany. The Bretons had been in rebellion against him since the previous autumn, and John now exacted his revenge, invading the duchy and laying it to waste. His mercenaries destroyed the city of Dol, burning down the cathedral and carrying off its relics.[11]

Philip, however, refused to be distracted. While John was busy harrying the Bretons, the French king's engineers were tightening their grip on Château Gaillard. Huge ditches were dug all the way round the castle on its landward side to prevent relief or escape. Along their length wooden forts were erected at regular intervals – seven in total, each surrounded by a ditch of its own, and filled with as many soldiers as it could hold. Philip himself, meanwhile, had left to attend to the siege of another of John's castles, Radepont, which he succeeded in taking in mid-September. Radepont lies just fifteen miles from Rouen.[12]

In early October, therefore, when John returned to his capital, it was to scenes of increasing chaos and despair. The city was said to be in flames at the time of his arrival (presumably due to an accident rather than enemy action) and the fire came close to destroying the ducal castle. This detail is provided by *The History of William Marshal*, a long biography of the famous warrior written in the 1220s, not long after his death. The *History* is one of our most valuable sources for John's reign but, like the chronicle of Roger of Wendover, it has to be used with caution. It was commissioned by the Marshal's family to defend his reputation, and at every turn seeks to disassociate him from King John. In its account of 1203, for example, it makes no mention at all of the Marshal's failed mission to relieve the Isle of Andely. It does, however, convey in vivid terms the growing desperateness of the situation in which the Marshal and his master found themselves that autumn.[13]

'Sire, listen to what I have to say,' says the Marshal after their return to Rouen. 'You haven't many friends.' The military situation, he explained, was becoming hopeless.

'Let any man who is afraid take flight!' replied the king. 'For I shall not flee this year.'

'I am well aware of that,' said the Marshal. 'I have not the slightest doubt about it. But you, sire, who are wise and powerful and of high birth, a man meant to govern us all, paid no attention to the first signs of discontent, and it would have been better for us all if you had.'[14]

This frank exchange made John predictably angry, and he shut himself away in his chamber. The next day he was nowhere to be found in the castle, and his men were annoyed to discover that he had slipped out of Rouen without them; they eventually caught up with him on the coast at Bonneville-sur-Touques, more than fifty miles away. For the rest of October, the king made similar rapid journeys around central and western Normandy, shoring up his remaining defences and doubtless trying to rally more support. But everywhere he went he was now dogged by fears of treachery. Returning to Rouen in November, he travelled by a deliberately indirect route; the main roads, he thought, were being watched by 'men who had no love for him'.[15]

Back in Rouen, John explained to his Norman followers that there was now only one solution: he must go to England, and persuade the barons there to come to Normandy's aid. Assuring his audience that this trip would be brief, he secretly sent his baggage on ahead to Bonneville. His own departure was equally furtive, for had become convinced that there was a plot among the Norman barons to hand him over to the king of France. With just a handful of trusted intimates, including William Marshal, John stole away from the city before daybreak. Travelling west by a circuitous route, he ultimately arrived at Barfleur, a port on the Cherbourg Peninsula, where a fleet to ferry him and his household across the Channel was waiting. The king sailed on 5 December. Most people, says the Marshal's biographer, suspected he would never return.[16]

2

The Family Empire

1120–1189

Eighty-three years earlier, almost to the day, another king had set sail from Barfleur in the direction of England. This was John's great-grandfather, Henry I.

Henry was the youngest son of William the Conqueror, and both king of England and duke of Normandy – the two countries had been yoked together by William's famous conquest of 1066. Since that momentous event, royal crossings of the Channel had become a matter of necessity and routine; William, for example, had made the voyage at least nineteen times during his twenty-one-year reign.[1] As this implies, it was not regarded as particularly risky, and Henry on this occasion made it across without incident. The king and his household set out from Barfleur at twilight on 25 November 1120, in calm and clear conditions, and arrived safe and sound in England the next morning.

But it soon became apparent that one ship from the royal fleet was missing. This was the so-called White Ship, a sleek new vessel that had been offered to Henry by its owner just before his departure, but which in the event had been left for the use of the more youthful members of the court. These young men and women had remained on shore as the rest of the royal entourage embarked, partying with the ship's crew and becoming increasingly merry. When they finally put to sea it was late and dark, and all of them were hopelessly drunk. Determined to overtake

14

the boats that had already left, they set out recklessly, and almost immediately struck a rock. The boat went down with the loss of all but one, who lived to tell the tale. Those who perished included many sons and daughters of the English aristocracy. They also included Henry I's son and heir, William.[2]

'No ship ever brought such misery to England', said one contemporary chronicler. When King Henry heard the news, says another, he fell to the ground, overcome with grief. It was not simply the loss of a child, devastating though that must have been – it was a dynastic catastrophe. Henry had fathered no fewer than twenty bastard children (the royal record), two of whom had also perished in the White Ship, but William had been his only legitimate son. The king, who had been a widower since the death of his queen, Matilda, two years earlier, wasted no time in trying to remedy the situation; barely a month later he married for a second time, taking a new young wife in the hope of producing a new male heir. But despite his best efforts, no more children were forthcoming. By the mid 1120s Henry was well into his fifties, and still without an obvious successor.[3]

And so the ageing king attempted to solve the problem in a different way, by fixing the succession on his only other legitimate child: his daughter, Matilda. Matilda had been married as a girl to the German emperor, but in 1125 she was newly widowed; Henry brought her back to England and lent on his leading men to accept her as his heir. The following year, to bolster Matilda's chances further, he arranged for her to be married to Geoffrey, son of the count of Anjou, a young man with the curious nickname 'Plantagenet'.* It was evidently Henry's hope that his daughter and her new husband would produce a son who would one day rule in his stead.[4]

---

* No one can say for certain why Geoffrey was called *Planta genista*, the Latin for 'broom plant'. None of his descendants used Plantagenet as a surname until it was adopted by Richard, duke of York, in 1460. But it remains a convenient and sometimes unavoidable way to describe the dynasty.[5]

And they did. In 1133 Matilda gave birth to her first child, and happily it was a boy, named Henry in honour of his royal grandfather. Young Henry would indeed grow up to inherit his grandfather's cross-Channel dominions, and much more besides. As King Henry II he would be the wonder of his age, greater in reputation than his grandfather: a successful warrior, a conscientious reformer, a maker of new laws and a builder of mighty castles. He would also be the father of King John.

But in 1133 all that lay in the distant future. In the meantime Henry had to obtain his inheritance, and that proved to be no easy task. Just two years after his birth his namesake grandfather died – his death famously said to have been caused by eating too many lampreys – and once the fearsome old king was gone his succession plan fell apart. Many of the barons who had sworn to support Matilda reneged on their oaths, and gave their support instead to her cousin, Stephen, who was crowned in December 1135, within days of Henry I's death. There followed a protracted period of civil war in England and Normandy as the supporters of each side slugged it out. For a few powerful men with flexible consciences and strong right arms it was a time of great opportunity; for everyone else it was a time of calamity and oppression. Contemporary authors complained of lawlessness, unlicensed castle-building and terrible unchecked violence. In the famous words of the Peterborough chronicler, 'men said openly that Christ and his saints slept'.[6]

Victory ultimately went to Matilda's party. In 1144 her husband Geoffrey, now count of Anjou, successfully wrested Normandy from Stephen's grasp, and five years later he granted it to his eldest son, the newly knighted Henry, just sixteen years old. At the start of 1153 Henry, now nineteen, invaded England, but with inconclusive results: the barons for the most part refrained from supporting either side, leading to a stalemate. It was only when Stephen's eldest son, Eustace, died that summer that the weary king agreed to recognize Henry as his heir. When Stephen himself died in October the following year, Henry peacefully succeeded him as king of England.[7]

Henry II, even at the start of his reign, was a much greater ruler than Stephen in every sense. Not only was he the undisputed ruler of both England and Normandy; he was also, since the death of his father in 1151, count of Anjou, which meant he ruled everything beyond Normandy's southern border to the valley of the Loire. Nor was that the limit of his power. In 1152 Henry had extended his rule even further, becoming the duke of Aquitaine, a vast territory that stretched from Anjou's southern border to the Pyrenees. He had obtained this massive windfall by marrying one of the most celebrated women in European history, Eleanor of Aquitaine.

The marriage of Henry and Eleanor has become the stuff of legend and romance, talked about and written about from their day until our own. For modern audiences, mention of their names together tends to evoke images from the 1968 film *The Lion in Winter*, in which Eleanor was played by Katharine Hepburn and Henry by Peter O'Toole. Picturing the real Henry is comparatively easy, thanks to several contemporary pen portraits which agree in their main details. He is described as being a little taller than average, red-haired, freckled and broad-chested, with a tendency to corpulence, despite constant exercise and a frugal diet. In Eleanor's case we are not so lucky: beyond describing her as beautiful, chroniclers give us no idea of her appearance. Nor do we have any physical remains to help us out. Both Henry and Eleanor were buried in Fontevraud Abbey in France, but their bones were lost when the abbey was sacked in the sixteenth century. We do still have the effigies that were originally placed on top of their tombs, and in Henry's case his likeness accords broadly with the descriptions provided by the chronicles. Eleanor's effigy, therefore, may also be an approximation of her likeness, but no more. The queen was over eighty when she died, yet her effigy clearly represents a much younger woman. It is best regarded as an idealised image of a queen rather than an attempt to portray an individual.[8]

Whatever her physical attributes, Eleanor's position as a great heiress made her irresistibly attractive. Probably born in 1122, she had suddenly inherited the duchy of Aquitaine in 1137 when her father, Duke William X, died unexpectedly while on pilgrimage, leaving no son to succeed him. Aquitaine was a mighty prize, covering perhaps a third of modern France, and so Eleanor became a highly desirable bride. Within a few months she was married to Louis, the son of the king of France, who one week later succeeded to the French throne as Louis VII. Their marriage, however, was not destined to last. Apart from being a similar age (Louis was about two years older) they appear to have had little in common, and when they went on crusade in 1147, malicious tongues whispered that Eleanor had seen rather too much of her uncle, Raymond of Antioch. Certainly by the time of their return from the east in 1149 the king and queen's marital problems were public knowledge, with even the pope encouraging them to start sleeping together again. The deciding factor was probably the fact that, after fifteen years of increasingly unhappy wedlock, they had produced two daughters but no sons. In March 1152 Louis had their union annulled.[9]

Eight weeks later, Eleanor married Henry. Although this marriage is often described as a love match in modern accounts, there is no reason to suppose that the motives of Eleanor's second husband were any less hard-nosed than those of her first. Aquitaine was still a great prize, and by marrying Eleanor Henry became its new duke. The question was whether he would be able to hang on to it. Henry was only nineteen at the time, but Eleanor was thirty. If her second marriage, like her first, failed to produce any sons, then Henry's claim to Aquitaine would last only for his own lifetime, and the duchy would pass to Eleanor's daughters, who remained in Louis' custody. The French king was not happy about his former wife's swift remarriage, but in divorcing her he was evidently prepared to gamble that no more children would be forthcoming.

Louis was set to be disappointed. Henry and Eleanor went on to have many children together – at least eight whose names are known to us. Their first child, born a year after their marriage, was a boy, named William in the long tradition of Aquitainian dukes, and three more boys followed by the end of the 1150s. Aquitaine was clearly going to pass to Henry's heirs.[10]

During these early years of his reign there was much else to keep Henry occupied. England and Normandy were both battered from years of civil war, and their great men had grown accustomed to doing as they liked in their own locales. Henry reversed this situation, restoring royal and ducal authority and taming the power of his magnates, sometimes destroying or confiscating their castles, and building new ones of his own such as Scarborough, Newcastle and Orford. A vigorous, intelligent and aggressive ruler, he moved like lightning across his vast demesnes as circumstances demanded, prompting some to comment that he must fly rather than travel by horse or ship. 'He was ever on his travels', wrote the cleric Walter Map, 'covering distances like a courier, and showing no mercy to his household.' And Henry's household was massive. Because of the sprawling empire he had assembled, he was the richest ruler in Europe, and in consequence he had the largest entourage. 'No such court like it has ever been heard of in the past,' said Walter, 'nor is likely to be feared again in the future.'[11]

This was the world into which John was born, probably around Christmas 1166 – or possibly 1167. The uncertainty arises because his birth occurred towards the end of the year, and because those few chroniclers who bothered to record it did so in lackadaisical terms. As Henry and Eleanor's eighth or ninth child – and, as it turned out, their last – John was not very important, at least from a political point of view. That much was made clear within a year or so of his arrival by the succession scheme devised by his father. Henry's plan, revealed in a peace treaty with Louis VII in 1169, was that on his death his extensive dominions would be divided. His firstborn son, William, had died as an infant, leaving a younger brother, Henry, born in 1155, as the eldest surviving child. Young Henry, it was envisaged, would inherit his father's patrimony – England, Normandy and Anjou. Aquitaine, which had been acquired by marriage, was to pass to the second surviving son, Richard, born in 1157, while a third son, Geoffrey, born in 1158, would receive the duchy of Brittany, which Henry II had obtained by force in 1166. But beyond that Henry had no more provinces to parcel out. For John there was, at present, no provision.[12]

There was very likely an element of prudence in this omission. The sons Henry had included in his planned division had all survived the perils of infancy and were entering adolescence and early manhood. John, by contrast, was still little more than a baby, and might well follow his eldest brother to an early grave. Yet John was also treated differently to his older siblings in another respect. As far as we can determine, it seems that Henry, Richard and Geoffrey, along with their older sisters, were raised in England. In 1160 the archbishop of Canterbury had written to Henry II, then on the Continent, suggesting that the king might consider returning to England at some point, since it would (among other things) enable him to see his children. As this implies, the older children did not get to spend much time with their father. They probably did, however, get to spend at least some time with their mother. Eleanor also had to travel, of course, but her constant childbearing in the 1150s and early 1160s must have meant her itinerary was less hectic than that of her husband, and her govern-mental duties seem to place her in England for most of this period. Certainly later in life Eleanor's older children were to demonstrate a closer attachment to her than to Henry.[13]

In John's case, however, matters were different. In 1168, now that Eleanor's childbearing days were over, Henry decided he could usefully redeploy her to govern Aquitaine. By this stage her older sons were sufficiently grown up to be learning the ropes of govern-ment. Henry and Geoffrey probably remained attached to their father's side; Richard, who was destined to rule Aquitaine, stayed with his mother and followed her south. But John had no such ropes to learn, and in any case was not old enough to accompany either of his parents as they executed their political responsibilities. Instead, he was left at Fontevraud Abbey in Anjou, to be raised by its community of nuns. He was not completely cut off from his family. His sister Joan, born in 1165 and thus a year or so older, was left at the abbey at the same time, and one of Henry's cousins, Matilda of Flanders, was a member of the community there. It is also possible that his mother could have made occasional visits – Poitiers is about a hundred miles from Fontevraud. Nevertheless, the permanent placement of John and Joan at the abbey suggests that both children probably saw a lot less of their mother than had been the case with their elder siblings.[14]

Harsh as this sounds as a childcare solution, there were good reasons for keeping toddlers in the safety of the cloister and away from the turbulent world of the court. In 1169, not long after her return to Aquitaine, Eleanor narrowly escaped an ambush by rebellious barons, in which her principal adviser, the earl of Salisbury, was killed. Then, in 1170, Henry committed the most notorious act of his reign by speaking the angry words that led four of his knights to murder the archbishop of Canterbury, Thomas Becket. The crime shocked all of Europe, and for a time Henry feared it would cost him his throne, as rival rulers urged the pope to excommunicate him and license their invasion of his lands. In the event the pope did neither, but the king remained a pariah until the spring of 1172, when papal legates finally absolved him as he knelt in penance outside the doors of Avranches Cathedral.[15]

Henry in fact remained in great danger, though he was slow to see it coming. Part of the problem was his increasingly strained relationship with his eldest son. The precise causes of their quarrel are now impossible to determine, but one factor was clearly the younger Henry's lack of independent power – the perennial complaint of heirs apparent down the ages. In 1170 the king had arranged for Henry to be crowned as an associate ruler – a common practice in France, but without precedent in England – from which point contemporaries referred to them as the Old King and the Young King. But it soon became evident that, despite his new title, the Young King had no real authority. He was given no lands of his own to manage, and hence had no independent income, while the membership of his household continued to be controlled by his father. Tellingly, the seal made for his use after 1170 depicts him without a sword. It is also possible that the young Henry harboured some resentment over the death of Thomas Becket, in whose household he had for a time been raised. It was certainly in revenge for Becket's death that the Young King claimed to be acting when he rose against his father in rebellion.[16]

The immediate cause of this rebellion, however, was the favour the Old King had shown to his youngest son. By 1172, it seems, Henry had become conscious of his initial failure to make any territorial provision for John. Within a decade or so, we find chroniclers referring to the boy as 'Lack-land' (Sans Terre), and suggesting that it was a nickname bestowed upon him by his father. True or not, towards the end of the year Henry set out to make good the deficiency, and arranged for John to be married to the daughter (and heir) of the count of Savoy. When the two rulers met in Limoges early in 1173, the count asked what lands his future son-in-law would bring to the marriage, and Henry responded, apparently spontaneously, that John would receive a trio of important castles in Anjou – Chinon, Loudun and Mirebeau. This proved too much for the Young King, who protested that his father had no right to make grants of land in Anjou without his agreement, and complained about his lack of power in general. When his protests and complaints were ignored, the Young King slipped away from his father's court at night, and rode to Paris to join Louis VII.[17]

Louis was a natural choice of ally for Henry II's disaffected offspring. Not only was he the Old King's main rival; he was also (and somewhat ironically) the Young King's father-in-law. Back in 1158 Louis and Henry had attempted to cement one of their periodic attempts at peace by arranging the betrothal of their infant children. Two years later, the young Henry, then aged four, had been married to Margaret, Louis' eldest daughter from his second marriage, then aged two. Neither the marriage nor the peace treaty was a great success, but it did draw the Young King into Louis' confidence, and make him a useful tool for French schemes against his father.[18]

Important as Louis was in encouraging the Young King's opposition, there is little doubt that the true instigator of the boy's rebellion was his mother. As soon as Henry II's back was turned, Eleanor of Aquitaine dispatched her other teenaged sons, the fifteen-year-old Richard and the fourteen-year-old Geoffrey, to join forces with their brother in Paris, while she herself rallied the barons of Poitou. This was an astonishing development. Contemporaries could (and did) note countless examples of sons rebelling against their fathers, but for a queen to rebel against her husband was unprecedented. Eleanor's reasons for doing so are necessarily speculative. Henry, who had just turned forty, had many mistresses throughout his career, so some commentators have supposed that the queen, now around fifty, was motivated by sexual jealousy. Others have suggested that Aquitaine itself was the key to the queen's displeasure, arguing that she and her Poitevin supporters had come to fear Henry's succession scheme, which made the duchy subordinate to the ruler of Normandy and England.[19]

Whatever the reason, by 1173 Eleanor of Aquitaine had reached the remarkable decision to rebel against her second husband in alliance with her first, and with her sons as co-conspirators. Nor was that the limit of the conspiracy. Right across Henry II's empire, others were ready to rise up against him. Nobles in England, Normandy and Anjou, still chafing at the losses they had suffered as a result of the king's masterful rule, rebelled in the hope of reversing them. Neighbouring rulers – the counts of Boulogne and Flanders, the king of Scotland – piled into the fray in expectation of territorial gain. It was a formidable, co-ordinated challenge on all fronts – the greatest crisis of Henry II's reign.

The Old King managed to ride out the storm. In part this was down to his superior resources: Henry was probably richer than all of his opponents put together, and he used his great wealth to recruit mercenaries in large numbers. In part it was due to his superior skills as a warrior and a politician. Henry knew when to sit tight and rely on trusted deputies, and when one of his legendary dashes would be decisive. In part it was down to luck. When his sons launched an attack on Normandy in the summer of 1173, their ally the count of Boulogne was killed by a crossbow bolt and the invasion collapsed; when the king of Scots invaded northern England the following summer,

he was taken by surprise by loyalist forces and captured. In the
latter case contemporaries saw divine providence at work, for the
Scottish king was seized even as Henry was submitting to a
penitential flogging by the monks of Canterbury for his role in
the death of Thomas Becket. When the king returned to the
Continent the following month the rebellion finally collapsed,
and his remaining enemies sued for peace.[20]

Henry was for the most part magnanimous in victory. His
eldest sons, if they did not achieve the autonomy they craved,
were nevertheless appeased with larger allowances. The Young
King was promised 15,000 pounds a year of Angevin money
(about £4,000 sterling) and received two castles in Normandy.
Richard was given two residences (apparently unfortified) in
Poitou and half its annual revenues. Geoffrey received half the
revenues of Brittany.[21]

But the biggest winner was the youngest son. In the first half
of 1174, while the rebellion was still happening, John was removed
from Fontevraud by his father and brought to England, to be
raised thereafter in the royal household. Now seven years old, he
had reached an age at which he would in any case have been
expected to start learning the sort of skills that nuns did not
normally teach, such as horsemanship and how to handle weapons.
Moreover, once the rebellion was finally over, John was given a
substantial endowment. It included the three castles in Anjou that
had been the immediate cause of his brothers' rebellion, plus
1,000 Angevin pounds a year. In addition he received a similar
sum from Normandy's revenues and two of the duchy's castles,
while in England he was granted even greater gifts: the castle
and county of Nottingham, the castle and lordship of Marlborough,
and an annual payment of £1,000 sterling. Henry also reserved
the right to grant to John any future English lands that might
revert to the Crown on the death of their owners. All of these
lands and revenues were at the expense of the Young King's
inheritance. It did not amount to a province to call his own, but
after 1174 John could no longer be said to lack land.[22]

By way of stark contrast, the big loser from the failed rebellion was Eleanor of Aquitaine. The queen had been captured in the autumn of 1173, reportedly disguised as a man, trying to reach her sons in Paris. Early in 1174 Henry escorted her to England, where she became his prisoner. For Eleanor there was to be no forgiveness. The following year the king tried to persuade the pope to have his marriage annulled, with the plan of forcing the queen into the abbey of Fontevraud as a nun. When the pope rejected this scheme, Henry settled for keeping her permanently confined, probably in the royal castle at Salisbury (now Old Sarum). In the meantime, he began to consort openly with his favourite mistress, Rosamund Clifford.[23]

How John might have reacted to his mother's imprisonment, given his apparently limited contact with her, is open to question. But Eleanor's older sons were clearly unhappy about her treatment: they, for instance, are also said to have objected vociferously to the planned divorce. That Henry, Richard and Geoffrey were close to their mother as children, or at least closer to her than to their father, is strongly implied by their willingness to join her in rebellion. By keeping Eleanor confined, however comfortably, the Old King was now effectively holding the queen hostage for her sons' good behaviour. It was an arrangement that might result in compliance, but one unlikely to foster genuine love or loyalty.[24]

Despite the obvious tensions between Henry II and his sons, they succeeded in co-operating in the years that followed. There was much work to be done in reversing the effects of the great rebellion. Henry himself devoted his efforts to England and Normandy, seizing and destroying the castles of former rebels; Richard and Geoffrey were dispatched to govern their respective provinces of Aquitaine and Brittany. For Henry the Young King there was less to do while his father remained in charge, so he devoted himself to the tournament circuit, winning many friends and admirers in the process. Periodically all three elder sons were recalled to attend their father's court at great festivals such as Easter and Christmas, and occasionally we also catch sight of John on such occasions. While they were able to work together in this way, the family proved to be unbeatable. In the summer of 1182, for instance, when Richard faced difficulty subduing a fresh rebellion in Aquitaine, his father came to his aid, along with Geoffrey and Henry the Young King, and together they easily brought the rebels to submission.[25]

Immediately after this, however, they again fell out, the source of contention once more the frustrations of the eldest son. Now twenty-seven, yet still without any meaningful power, the younger Henry approached his father in the autumn of 1182 and asked again for a portion of his inheritance – Normandy, or another territory 'from which he might be able to support knights in his service'. As in 1173, Henry II refused, with almost identical consequences: the Young King took himself off to the court of the French king.[26]

The difference on this occasion was that it was no longer the court of Louis VII. The old French king had suffered a stroke in the summer of 1179 and died the following year at the age of sixty. Into his place had stepped his fifteen-year-old son, Philip. From the moment of his birth, Philip – the future Philip Augustus – had carried a great weight of expectation on his shoulders. It had taken Louis three marriages and almost thirty years, but at last in August 1165 he had succeeded in fathering a son. The citizens of Paris had rung bells and lit bonfires in celebration, declaring 'By the grace of God there is born to us this night a king who shall be a hammer to the king of the English.' This was the reminiscence of a later chronicler, writing with the benefit of hindsight. Henry II for his part had endeavoured to cultivate good relations with Philip; by 1182 he and his sons had already intervened several times to assist the new French king in establishing his rule. But this initial help earned Henry little in the way of long-term gratitude. As Philip became his own man it became clear that his main policy would be to destroy the power of his Plantagenet neighbours.[27]

The Young King's trip to Paris in the autumn of 1182 turned out to be of only short duration. His father, worried that fresh filial disaffection could lead to another general revolt, quickly wooed him back with the promise of an increased allowance. At

Christmas the Old King celebrated by summoning all his sons to Caen for what the chroniclers describe as the greatest court of his reign, with more than 1,000 knights reportedly in attendance. During the festivities, however, the tensions within the family exploded. Henry II, perhaps in the hope of further mollifying the Young King, attempted to formalize the future relationship between his various dominions, and demanded that both Geoffrey and Richard do homage to their elder brother – that is, to kneel before him, place their hands within his hands, and promise to be 'his man'. Geoffrey obliged, but Richard refused: his older brother, he objected, was no better than he. Eventually Richard was won round, and agreed to go through with the ceremony, provided that his right to hold Aquitaine was guaranteed. But this was a guarantee that the Young King was unable to give because – as he now revealed – he was in league with the Aquitainian rebels whom they had collectively crushed the previous summer. Young Henry, it seems, was plotting to replace Richard.[28]

Henry II imperiously ordered his sons to swear peace to each other, and sent Geoffrey to arrange a conference with the rebels. But here the plot grew thicker still when Geoffrey, on meeting Richard's enemies, promptly joined them. Henry's court broke up in confusion. The Young King set out for Aquitaine to assist Geoffrey and the rebels, Richard to try to suppress them. Their father gave orders to raise an army and set out in pursuit.

A violent stand-off between the two sides followed, which lasted throughout the whole of the spring of 1183, and started to draw in the rulers of other regions, to the extent that it seemed certain to become a rerun of the great rebellion of ten years earlier. What stopped it escalating in this way was the sudden death of the Young King, who fell sick with dysentery while pillaging along the Dordogne, and died on 11 June. His father, who had suspected that reports of his son's illness were just another ruse, was reportedly struck down with grief when he discovered the truth. Whatever his faults, the Young King had been a popular figure, praised by contemporaries as the epitome of chivalry, and much loved by Henry II.[29]

At the same time, one less son might be seen to be a blessing, politically, for a king who seemed to have too many. The Young King had died without any children, so his death presented Henry with an opportunity to revise his plan for the succession. Richard, now the eldest surviving son, would take the place of his dead brother as heir to the patrimony – Anjou, Normandy and England. In return he would surrender Aquitaine to John, who would at last obtain a province of his own. Geoffrey, who had ended his rebellion in the summer, remained duke of Brittany, but was deprived from holding its castles.

But when Henry summoned his sons to Normandy in the autumn of 1183 to announce this plan, Richard made his feelings very clear. After obtaining a few days' grace to consult his advisers, he rode off at night back to his duchy, sending messengers to tell his father that he would never give it up. This might seem perverse: England, Normandy and Anjou together appear to constitute a greater prize than Aquitaine. But Richard had been linked with Aquitaine since his mother's return to the duchy in 1168. In 1172, at the age of fourteen, he had been formally invested as its duke, and since that time he had enjoyed – and, moreover, fought hard for – real political power. To accept his father's new scheme would mean giving up that power in exchange for the empty role his elder brother had found so frustrating.[30]

Since Richard was so well entrenched in Aquitaine, Henry's initial reaction was moderate: throughout the winter of 1183–4 he tried to win his son round with promises and reasoned argument. But eventually, faced with Richard's continued obstinacy, the king snapped, and angrily ordered John to seize the duchy by force. As in the case of Thomas Becket, it is debatable whether Henry really meant what he said, for John had no resources to attack Richard, nor did Henry lend him any. When the king crossed the Channel to England in June 1184, however, John did indeed invade Aquitaine, with the help of his brother Geoffrey. Since John was only seventeen years old and Geoffrey twenty-six, we may suspect the initiative lay with the elder brother. This was John's first political action, but Geoffrey had been playing these kinds of power games for many years. Contemporaries were aware of his skill in manipulating others, and condemned him for it. He was, said one, 'overflowing with words, smooth as oil, possessed, by his syrupy and persuasive eloquence, of the power of dissolving the apparently indissoluble, able to corrupt two kingdoms with his tongue, of tireless endeavour and a hypocrite in everything'. 'Geoffrey, that son of treachery,' said another, 'that son of iniquity.'[31]

The joint offensive of John and Geoffrey was not very effective, and Richard, rather than confronting his brothers head-on, responded by laying waste to Geoffrey's lands in Brittany. But when their father heard that his sons were once again at war he commanded them all to come to England. It is a mark of Henry's continuing authority that all three obeyed, but perhaps a mark of his desperation that, in advance of their arrival, he released their mother from captivity. Eleanor, now in her sixties, is known to have attended council meetings at the end of 1184, and so it may have been as a result of her influence that a public reconciliation between her sons was achieved that December. As subsequent events would show, nothing in reality had been settled regarding the succession, but Henry was apparently willing to leave Richard in possession of Aquitaine for now. That much was made clear from his sudden revival of a long-nurtured plan to make John king of Ireland.[32]

Ireland was the last significant addition to Henry II's sprawling empire. Before his accession it had largely avoided the successive waves of conquerors that had swept over the rest of the British Isles. Neither the Romans nor the Anglo-Saxons, nor even the Norman kings of England, had attempted to extend their power across the Irish Sea. The Vikings had settled there, but only in a handful of coastal towns. For the most part, Ireland remained what it had always been: a Celtic country, whose inhabitants, though they might trade with their English neighbours, owed no allegiance to England's kings.[33]

All this changed in the time of Henry II. The king had apparently contemplated a conquest of Ireland at the very start of his reign. Although he had been discouraged by his mother – and was anyway soon distracted by more pressing concerns on the Continent – he had been supported by the Church, who regarded the Irish as a backwards and barbarous people, Christian only in name, with reprehensible attitudes towards sex and marriage. Divorce was available on demand, concubinage was commonplace, and the line between bastardy and legitimacy so thin as to be non-existent. Leaving the strictures of the Church aside, these relaxed attitudes meant that Irish politics, based as they were on rival dynasties, were wont to be turbulent. Ireland was a land of many kings – as many kings as elsewhere there were earls, explained one English observer – locked in a ceaseless round of competition. They competed in part for the distinction of being recognized as the country's 'high-king', but this title was purely honorific, and brought nothing in the way of administrative power. Power in Ireland was based on tribute and military might.[34]

It was these turbulent politics that had ultimately drawn in Henry II. In 1166 the king of Leinster, Dermot MacMurrough, had been driven from his lands in south-east Ireland by his rival, the king of Connacht. His first instinct was to seek help from his powerful English neighbour, but Henry, preoccupied with affairs in Aquitaine, was unenthusiastic. Instead, with Henry's licence, Dermot turned to the Anglo-Norman lords of south Wales: men who had long experience of fighting against Celtic foes by virtue of living on a hostile frontier. In return for the promise of new lands, some of these men crossed to Ireland with Dermot in 1167 and helped him recover part of his patrimony. Cutting-edge techniques and technology – cavalry charges, crossbows and castles – gave them the military advantage over the Irish, and their material gains soon encouraged more adventurers to follow in their wake. Eventually, in August 1170, they were joined by Richard fitz Gilbert, known to posterity as 'Strongbow', a former earl who had lost his title by supporting King Stephen. In return for supporting Dermot he demanded the Irish king's daughter in marriage, along with the right to succeed him after his death. Thus when Dermot obligingly died the following year, it was fitz Gilbert who had stepped into his shoes as Leinster's ruler.[35]

At this point Henry II had decided to intervene in person. It was one thing for his vassals to act as swords for hire and win new lands; quite another for one of them to set himself up as an independent power. In October 1171 the king sailed to Ireland, bringing with him his splendid court, and a large army, to overawe both the native Irish lords and the new English settlers. There was no fighting: Richard fitz Gilbert submitted at once and received Leinster back as a fief. Many Irish rulers also submitted to Henry, acknowledging him as their new overlord. The net effect of the king's intervention, however, was to leave Ireland in a state of limbo. The settlers would later complain that his action had robbed the conquest of its momentum, giving the Irish a chance to recover and fight back. After his departure in April 1172, the country entered into a state of almost constant war between the natives and the newcomers. Henry attempted to make peace with the Irish in 1175, but the English settlers had no interest in observing its terms. In Ireland, the castle-building, colonisation and conflict continued.[36]

It was against this background, perhaps in the hope of a fresh start, that Henry had earmarked Ireland as a suitable prospect for his youngest son. In 1177, in a council meeting at Oxford, he made extensive grants of Irish land to new settlers and had them recognize John as the country's future king. At that time John was only ten years old, so his interest in Ireland had to be upheld by deputies. Before his departure in 1172 Henry had granted the Irish kingdom of Meath to Hugh de Lacy, another baron from the Welsh borders, intending that he should act as a counterweight to Richard fitz Gilbert. But after fitz Gilbert's death in 1176, Hugh de Lacy himself had begun to seem too tall a poppy. When he married the daughter of the Irish king of Connacht, people began to speculate that he was scheming to take the kingship of Ireland for himself.[37]

The plan to send John to Ireland seems to have been shelved in 1183, when the death of the Young King prompted Henry II to think in terms of a more general reshuffle. Now that it had proved impossible to dislodge Richard from Aquitaine, however, the original plan was resumed. In the summer of 1184 Henry sent new officials to Ireland to prepare the ground for John's arrival. These preparations culminated on 31 March 1185 when the king knighted his son at Windsor Castle, the symbolic conferral of arms signifying that John, now aged eighteen, was old enough to wield power in his own right.[38] How enthusiastic he was about wielding power in Ireland is open to doubt. Two weeks earlier, during a council in London, he had reportedly begged his father to allow him to go to the Holy Land instead. Since the start of the year the patriarch of Jerusalem had been at Henry's court, trying to obtain military support for the beleaguered Christian communities in Palestine, and had identified John as a potential leader. But Henry had refused their imprecations. Within days of his knighting at Windsor John was dispatched into south Wales, where a company of 300 knights and an even larger force of soldiers and archers were waiting to accompany him across the Irish Sea. On 24 April they set sail from Milford Haven in a fleet of sixty ships, landing safely at Waterford at noon the following day.[39]

The expedition was an unqualified disaster. The contemporary chronicler Gerald of Wales, who travelled in John's company at Henry's request, explains how their mission was compromised from the moment they disembarked. The new arrivals were met at Waterford by a great number of Irish lords – those native leaders who had accepted English authority and come to welcome John as their new ruler. But, says Gerald, the newcomers treated these men with contempt and derision, even to the extent of pulling their beards, 'which the Irish wore full and long, according to the custom of their country'. Having been humiliated, these Irishmen withdrew their allegiance, and convinced others who had been contemplating submission to do the same. John, they told their fellow countrymen, was a mere boy, surrounded by others almost as young, who were interested only in juvenile pursuits. Under his leadership there was no hope of Ireland enjoying peace and security.[40]

To some extent, the behaviour of John's party was only to be expected. They had not come to Ireland to reach an accommodation with the natives – Henry II had abandoned that policy back in 1177. Gerald says that John also alienated the formerly loyalist Irish lords by granting out their lands to his own followers, and this is confirmed by his surviving charters. John's mistake lay not so much in provoking those whom he expected would be his enemies, as in simultaneously aggravating those whom he assumed would be his allies. The Anglo-Norman lords from south Wales who had founded the colony a generation earlier also weighed up their new lord's behaviour and found it wanting. Having goaded the native Irish into outright hostility, John and his coterie were said by Gerald to have spent most of their time in the towns on the coast, indulging in riotous living, leaving the settler communities of the interior to fend for themselves against Irish attacks. Gerald is doubtless exaggerating here; his bitterness at John's failure was personal, for he hailed from one of these same pioneering settler families. John's charters prove that he spent at least some time on the marches of his lordship, and Irish annalists report that he established three new castles to stake out claims to further territory. When the garrisons of these castles carried out raids into neighbouring Irish lands, however, they were defeated and slaughtered. Others among John's army reportedly deserted to the Irish side because he refused to pay them properly. By the end of the year, his forces were so depleted that he was forced to return to England.[41]

During John's absence in Ireland the struggle between his brothers Richard and Geoffrey had continued, with a fresh round of fighting in Anjou. At the root of their rivalry was Henry II's obstinate refusal, since the death of the Young King, to provide any clarity on the issue of the succession. Henry appears to have wanted to keep everyone in the dark, especially Richard, and to have encouraged the hopes of Geoffrey. Back in December 1183, for example, when Richard had been in open defiance over Aquitaine, Henry had reached a new agreement with Philip Augustus over the Vexin, a strip of territory on the Franco-

Norman frontier that had been in dispute for over a century. The two kings had agreed it would become the dowry of Philip's sister, Alice, and would pass to whichever of Henry's sons she married. The 'whichever' was highly significant, because Alice had already been betrothed for the past fifteen years to Richard. The new note of ambiguity implied that he might not inherit Normandy, and perhaps not England or Anjou either.[42]

Soon after John's return from Ireland, however, the pendulum swung perceptibly in Richard's favour. In March 1186 Henry and Philip met to confirm the Vexin agreement, but this time it was specifically stated that Alice would marry Richard. Now it was Geoffrey's turn to take umbrage, since this seemed to indicate the decline of his own prospects. Like the Young King before him, he took off to Paris, where he began to plot with Philip. The French king obligingly bestowed upon him the title 'steward of France', an honour traditionally held by the rulers of Anjou, indicating that Geoffrey's thoughts were now bending in that direction.[43]

As for John, Henry's intention was still very much to make him king of Ireland. The new pope, elected at the end of 1185, proved to be more enthusiastic about the plan than his predecessor, and had promised to send a gold crown with peacock feathers for the coronation ceremony. Then, in the summer of 1186, even more propitious news arrived. Hugh de Lacy, the tall poppy whom both John and Henry had regarded as an obstacle to their ambitions in Ireland, was dead, felled by a native Irish axe. On hearing this Henry was reportedly jubilant, and made immediate preparations for his son's return. A new expedition was hastily assembled at Chester and John was dispatched north to join it. He was waiting for a favourable wind to cross the Irish Sea when messengers arrived to tell him of another death. Geoffrey had been killed in a tournament in Paris on 19 August.

This startling news changed everything. At his father's command John returned south at once, sending a deputy across the Irish Sea in his stead. Ireland was suddenly a peripheral concern, the crown of peacock feathers redundant. New and much wider vistas now opened up to him. Geoffrey, not without Henry's encouragement, had been angling for a greater share of his father's inheritance. John now stepped naturally into that role. Geoffrey had died leaving two daughters but no sons; Richard was still unmarried and constantly engaged in the risky business of warfare. In the summer of 1186, John found himself in the exhilarating position of being a single heartbeat from the succession to all his father's dominions.[44]

The rivalry that this created between John and Richard was not immediately apparent, thanks to the precipitate action of Philip Augustus. Deprived of his leverage by the loss of Geoffrey, the French king demanded the surrender of Brittany and the dead duke's daughters, threatening war if Henry refused to comply. Talks during the autumn produced only a short truce, and in January 1187 Philip invaded the Vexin. Further talks in the spring led to a second truce until midsummer, at which point Philip invaded Berry, another contested region, east of Anjou. In the face of this new aggression, the fractious Plantagenets pulled together. John and Richard joined forces in Berry to hold the town of Châteauroux against Philip, and when the French king besieged them there, Henry marched to their relief. For a moment it looked as if the argument might be settled in the fields outside Châteauroux by a decisive battle, but in the event (as indeed happened on most occasions during the Middle Ages) neither side was truly ready to take such an enormous risk. Instead, after two weeks of protracted talks, a third truce was agreed, this time for two years.[45]

But as soon as the truce was sealed, dissension among the Plantagenets erupted once more, when Richard surprised everyone by riding back to Paris with Philip. 'Between the two of them,' wrote the well-informed courtier Roger of Howden, 'there grew up so great an affection that King Henry was much alarmed.' The fact that Howden, in describing this sudden affection, mentions that Philip and Richard shared the same bed has led some modern commentators to assume that they were having a homosexual affair, which was almost certainly not the case. Determining sexuality at a distance of 800 years is, of course, difficult, but 'sharing a bed' for medieval writers was a typical expression of friendship rather than erotic love. Richard's sexual preferences are probably better inferred by Howden's comment elsewhere that the men of Aquitaine disliked their duke because he abducted 'their wives, daughters and kins-women by force, and made them his concubines'.[46]

What alarmed Henry II in 1187 was not reports of his son sleeping with another man, but the political alliance this act implied. First the Young King, then Geoffrey, now Richard: Philip had beguiled one brother after another and turned them against their father. The likeliest explanation for this latest defection is that, during the final round of peace talks, Philip had played on Richard's fears that Henry was planning to cut him out of the succession, and aiming to pass England, Anjou and Normandy to John. Certainly this was the rumour that circulated among contemporary chroniclers, who were in no doubt about the balance of Henry's paternal affections. John was 'a son he loved and greatly trusted', said the biographer of William Marshal. 'The youngest son, John,' wrote William of Newburgh, 'he loved the most tenderly.' Richard, by contrast, had always been his mother's favourite, and events since 1183 had shown that there was little love lost between him and Henry. Soon after his visit to Paris, Richard raided his father's treasury at Chinon, using the proceeds to garrison his castles in Aquitaine. Such actions indicate the enormous distrust that existed between them.[47]

At length, by sending messengers to Richard with promises of redress, Henry induced him to return to his side; Richard admitted he had been led astray, and swore that in future he would remain faithful. But suspicion and ill will remained. Towards the end of the summer came the shocking news that the army of the crusader kingdom of Jerusalem had been wiped out in battle by Muslim forces led by the sultan Saladin. The Christian communities in the Holy Land, established nine decades earlier during the First Crusade, seemed to be on the point of extinction, and a few months later the people of western Europe heard the worst: Jerusalem itself had fallen. Richard responded at once, pledging to go on crusade by publicly taking the cross, much to the anger and alarm of his father, who saw that Richard's absence would delay any peace with Philip Augustus. As it was, by January 1188, the public mood was such that both Henry and Philip also felt obliged to take the cross. But now it was Richard's turn to be alarmed when Henry forbade John from doing the same. For what reason was John being held back, if not to usurp Richard's position?[48]

Despite the distrust, Henry and Richard were united in arms against Philip in August 1188, after fresh fighting broke out in Berry and along the Franco-Norman border. But, as before, the subsequent peace talks drew Richard and Philip into collaboration. In November, at Bonsmoulins in Normandy, they arrived together, and presented Henry with a proposal for peace. Philip would give up his recent territorial gains on two conditions: that Richard must marry Alice, and that Henry must make all his barons recognize Richard as his heir. When Henry refused, Richard took it as final confirmation of his long-nurtured fears. 'Now at last,' he said, 'I must believe what I had always thought was impossible.' So saying, Richard stunned his audience by turning to Philip and doing homage to the French king for Normandy, Anjou and Aquitaine.

It was the final break between father and son. Henry tried to woo Richard back as before, but without success. Attempts at further dialogue during the winter achieved nothing, and by the spring of 1189 both sides were readying themselves for war. At the end of May, at La Ferté-Bernard, not far from Le Mans, Richard and Philip repeated their demands for the marriage of Alice and the confirmation of the succession, adding that John must also take the cross and accompany Richard on crusade. John, for the most part invisible during these months, was still very much attached to his father's side.[49]

Henry again refused, at which point Philip and Richard launched their attack, seizing La Ferté-Bernard and a number of other castles nearby. Henry, who had retreated to Le Mans – his birthplace – was forced to flee as the city went up in flames, and came close to being captured by his attackers. The king at first headed north, towards the safety of Normandy, but only a few miles from the Norman border, to the consternation of his household, he decided to turn back in the direction of Anjou.

Henry was heading south to die. Although at fifty-six he was not particularly old, even by medieval standards, he was worn out from a lifetime in the saddle and the stresses of recent years. Already unwell the previous Christmas, his condition was no doubt made worse by the struggle against Richard during the spring. Now in the summer heat he fell ill again. By travelling on lesser roads and tracks he managed to reach Chinon, the castle of his Angevin ancestors, where he lay sick for a fortnight.

Meanwhile Richard and Philip were drawing ever closer, overrunning towns and castles in their path. When Tours capitulated on 3 July, Henry was obliged to rise from his bed to meet them, his attendants holding him upright on his horse as the terms of his surrender were dictated. In addition to agreeing to all of his adversaries' previous demands, Henry was now required to renew his allegiance to the French king, and pay him an indemnity of 20,000 marks. It was a humiliating end for a man who had been the greatest ruler in Christendom. As he leant forward to give Richard the required kiss of peace, says Gerald of Wales, Henry whispered in his son's ear, 'God grant that I may not die until I have had my revenge on you.'[50]

God was not nearly so generous. Too weak to ride, Henry was carried back to Chinon on a litter. As part of the terms of his surrender, the ailing king had agreed to receive back into his peace all those who had deserted him in recent weeks and joined forces with Richard and Philip. That night he asked to hear the list of their names, which his servants had been trying to keep from him. Henry insisted that they be read out, and received what several chroniclers believed to be the blow that killed him. 'Sire, so Jesus Christ help me,' said the vice chancellor, 'the first which is written down here is Lord John, your son.'[51]

3

Refusing to Rally

1204–1205

F ive months into the siege of Château Gaillard, Philip Augustus' patience was starting to wear thin.

The French king had known from the outset that taking the mighty castle would be difficult. Its lofty position and ingenious design meant that any direct assault would probably prove futile. Nor was it likely that in this instance the garrison could be bribed into submission. Commanders of other castles, if they were landholders in Normandy, had sought to hold on to their lands by dint of a well-timed defection. But Château Gaillard had been entrusted to Roger de Lacy, a man who had no estates in Normandy at all, only in England, and thus every reason to maintain his allegiance to King John. The enormous effort Philip had made to blockade the castle, ringing it with ditches and towers, shows that from the first he was anticipating that it would be necessary to starve the defenders into submission. As his chaplain William the Breton commented, 'It is cruel hunger alone that conquers the invincible.'[1]

At the start of the siege the prospects for a starvation strategy had seemed excellent, for Lacy had made a strategic blunder in admitting the townspeople of Little Andely. There may have been a strong emotional and moral case for doing so, for many of them were the friends and relatives of the garrison, but Lacy belatedly realized that these 'useless mouths' – a multitude of perhaps 2,000 people – were quickly going to consume the castle's carefully stockpiled provisions. In an attempt to undo his error, he started sending them out in groups, and initially the French forces allowed them to pass through the siege lines to safety. At length, however, Philip himself learned what was happening, and called a halt to the exodus. When the final group was sent out from the castle, they were met with a hail of arrows; when they fled back in terror, they found the castle gates had been mercilessly barred against them. Appalling scenes followed that winter as these unfortunates were left to starve in the no-man's-land between the two lines, seeking shelter under rocks, and eating herbs, dogs and – eventually – each other.[2]

Besides being pleased with himself on this score, Philip must have been greatly encouraged in December by the departure of King John. Those who noted his stealthy flight from Normandy and concluded that he would never return seemed to have the evidence on their side. At some point during the winter, Philip intercepted a letter from John, intended for Roger de Lacy, thanking the constable for his stalwart service, but making it clear that he and the rest of the garrison at Château Gaillard could expect no relief in the foreseeable future.[3]

As time wore on, however, Philip's confidence in playing the long game must have started to ebb. Christmas came and went, and January too, but still Lacy and his men showed no signs of weakening. As winter turned to spring the likelihood of a relief force landing from England increased. Towards the end of February, the French king (who had not been present for the duration) returned to take personal command of the siege. He allowed the surviving wretches outside the castle to leave, and gave orders that they be fed (though the sudden consumption of food caused many of them to die). Philip could now afford to be compassionate, for he had decided to risk a direct assault.

The only direction from which such an attack could conceivably be mounted was the south-east, where the rock on which Château Gaillard stood was joined to higher ground by a narrow neck of land. King Richard had recognized this weakness and

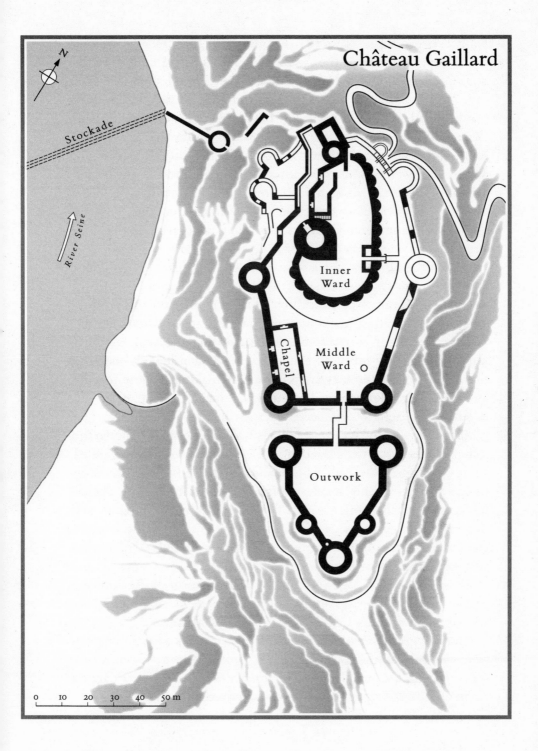

built a large outwork facing that direction, completely separate from the main part of the castle. This was where Philip chose to strike. His men levelled and widened the ground so that a giant siege tower could be rolled towards the edge of the castle's outer ditch, and then attempted to fill the ditch so that the tower could be positioned right up against the walls. When this proved too time-consuming they descended into the ditch using ladders and began scaling the other side, intending to undermine the castle's foremost tower. It must have been a deadly business with heavy casualties, but eventually the French king's sappers managed to bring the tower down. As it collapsed it partially filled the ditch, making it easier for the attackers to storm the breach. The defenders, realizing that the outwork was lost, set fire to its buildings and withdrew into the castle's middle ward.

The French now faced a ditch of similar size and the prospect of sustaining further losses in trying to cross it, until one of them spotted a potential Achilles heel. Against the south-west wall of the castle, high above the Seine, stood a chapel. This was not part of the original design, but had been added on John's orders the previous year. By edging around the outside of the walls and standing on each other's shoulders, a small group of men managed to reach the chapel's window, which was unbarred and unguarded. Once inside what turned out to be a locked room, they beat on its door to make a racket. The defenders, startled to discover their enemies were already inside, panicked and fell back for a second time, once again firing the part of the castle they had abandoned. Safe within the chapel's vaulted chamber, the intruders waited for the flames to subside, then emerged to lower the main drawbridge, allowing the rest of the French army to enter.

Roger de Lacy and his men, reduced in number and now confined to the castle's innermost ward, could probably not have held out for very much longer. As it was, another design flaw (in this case Richard's) greatly reduced their chances. Instead of a drawbridge over the final ditch there was a solid span of stone, under which Philip's miners were able to shelter and work unimpeded. In desperation the defenders dug a mine of their own and confronted their attackers in underground combat, but the consequence of all the tunnelling was to weaken the walls above. After a few shots from the French king's catapult, the walls collapsed. Heroically, Lacy and his men fought on, even as their enemies swarmed around them, eventually to be dragged out by their ankles. Thus Château Gaillard was taken, on 6 March 1204, after one of the longest and most bitterly fought sieges in European history.

At that moment John was travelling in the Midlands, returning south from a visit to York. Since his arrival in England the previous December, he had made some preparations for his promised return to Normandy. He must have summoned a council of magnates and bishops almost immediately, for they had assembled in Oxford in the first week of January, and agreed to grant him financial aid and military service. In February he had sent messengers to his subjects in Ireland asking them for similar assistance. Beyond that, however, evidence of preparation for the king's return is thin. Towards the end of February some provisions, men and money were sent across the Channel, perhaps provoked by the news that Château Gaillard was now under direct assault. But John clearly believed that the castle would continue to hold out for many more weeks. On 6 March itself, the very day of its fall, he gave orders for beasts to be trapped in the New Forest and shipped to Normandy, so that he would be assured of good hunting when he eventually arrived.[4]

News of Château Gaillard's fall must therefore have been received with shock. A council was held in London at the end of March, at which it was decided to dispatch an embassy to Philip Augustus, in the hope of persuading him to accept a peace. The ambassadors were high-ranking, including the archbishop of Canterbury, the bishops of Norwich and Ely, and two senior earls (one of whom was William Marshal), as well as a visiting papal legate. But the talks that took place in mid-April were predictably fruitless, for Philip had no reason to negotiate. 'King Philip did not want peace,' wrote a contemporary chronicler, Ralph of Coggeshall, 'because he was sure that he would get possession of all the king's land in a short time, and so he always proposed something that was unacceptable, or something that was not possible, in the completion of the peace agreement.'[5]

As soon as the meeting was over, Philip proceeded with his invasion. Rouen was his ultimate objective, but the city was well defended with a triple ring of ditches, and its citizens steadfast in their attachment to the Plantagenet cause. The French king therefore led his army into western Normandy, to pick off easier targets. Falaise, the birthplace of William the Conqueror, resisted for a week, before the mercenaries holding it calculated that they would be better off switching sides. Caen, where the Conqueror lay buried, put up no resistance at all, because (in Ralph of Coggeshall's words) 'they had no one strong enough to defend them'. Philip's army quickly overran the Cherbourg Peninsula, taking Barfleur and Cherbourg itself. And so it continued across the rest of the duchy, as men flocked to make peace with the French king and secure favourable terms.[6]

Against this background of general collapse, the resolve in Rouen began to crack. On 1 June the city's military commander, Peter de Préaux, struck a temporary truce with Philip, agreeing to surrender if no help arrived from England within thirty days. Desperate messages had already been sent to John, telling him 'if he did not come to save his lands he would lose the lot of them'. The biographer of William Marshal says that John immediately ordered an army to assemble at Portsmouth, but was thwarted by the lackadaisical attitude of his barons. 'Many of those summoned delayed for too long, at a time when delay was not the order of the day.' The official record, however, shows no sign of any serious military preparations at this point. Word must have been carried back to Rouen, as Roger of Wendover says, that no assistance was to be expected, and that the citizens would have to fend for themselves. On 24 June, a week before the truce was set to expire, Peter de Préaux surrendered his command, and Philip rode through the gates of the city in triumph. With the fall of the duchy's capital, the remaining castles and towns of Normandy also submitted.[7]

Nor was it just Normandy. While Philip had been attending to the conquest of the duchy, his allies had been busy seizing John's lands further south. Here the signal for collapse had been the death of John's mother, Eleanor of Aquitaine, on 1 April. 'A noble queen, indeed, and a spirited and wealthy lady' (as a London chronicler described her in an obituary), Eleanor was interred at Fontevraud alongside Henry II. Released from captivity after Henry's death in 1189, she had gone on to play a pivotal role during the reigns of both her surviving sons, not least because she continued to command the personal loyalty of many southern magnates. But this vestigial attachment to the Angevin cause died with her. In the spring of 1204, the barons of Poitou deserted en masse to the king of France, and in August Philip made a triumphal entry into Poitiers. By the end of the summer, all that remained of John's huge continental inheritance was the southern part of Aquitaine, and even here his grip was becoming extremely tenuous. Everything else, apart a few embattled castles in Anjou, had been conquered.[8]

Contemporaries were well aware that these were momentous events. 'Since Duke William, who conquered the kingdom of the English,' wrote Ralph of Coggeshall, 'the kings of England have always been dukes of Normandy, up to the time of King John, who in the fifth year of his reign lost the duchy, together with many other lands overseas.' One hundred and thirty-nine years of joint rule, observed Ralph, counting inclusively from 1066 to 1204, had come to a sudden end.[9]

There is no doubt that, as a result of this ignominious loss, John felt an immense burden of shame and guilt. He had lost the continental lands of his ancestors. These were not, as English historians of past generations have sometimes pretended, peripheral territories, which England's kings were well to be rid of. They were, on the contrary, the heartlands of the Plantagenet Empire – the patrimony. There was a reason why Henry II had gone south to die at Chinon, and why he and Richard I were buried in an abbey beside the banks of the Loire: ancestrally, even emotionally, these lands were home.

This was also the attitude of many of the people surrounding King John. Like all medieval men and women of any importance, John was the head of a great household – in his case, the greatest household in the country, with a permanent staff of several hundred. The majority of them were menials: huntsmen, porters, carters, grooms, cooks, stable lads, laundresses, and so on. But there were also plenty of high-status individuals attendant on the king: knights, esquires and senior clerks. Knights could act as advisers and diplomats in peacetime, and form the core of the army during war; clerks performed religious devotions and acted as the royal secretariat. Above and beyond this, however, these high-status individuals were the king's intimate companions – his counsellors, even his friends. They were the people always on hand to offer support and advice.

In the years leading up to 1204, John's inner counsellors had become dominated by one particular set of men: military captains and clerks from Anjou and, specifically, the region around Tours. These men, having sided with John and followed him back to England, had lost everything in the course of the French conquest. As such they were fiercely loyal to the king, for being landless exiles left them wholly dependent on his goodwill, and always looking to him for reward, whether in the form of new lands, money or offices. They were also, like John, wholeheartedly committed to winning back the continental lands they had lost.[10]

But what was the attitude to the loss of the Angevin Empire beyond John and his intimate counsellors? What, for instance, did the barons – the great men of England, whose ancestors had crossed with the Conqueror – think? Here the picture is more mixed, and there is debate among historians today, just as there was no doubt debate in baronial halls at the time. In some cases, such families no longer had any links with Normandy, having divided their English and Norman estates between different branches at some date before the disaster.[11] But in other cases, there were families who held substantial lands on both sides of the Channel right up to 1204, who were afterwards left nursing serious financial losses. (And even if the estates themselves were not hugely profitable, they might be considered important for reasons of sentiment or prestige.) William Marshal and his fellow negotiator, the earl of Leicester, had succeeded in striking a private deal with Philip Augustus during their pointless embassy in the spring of 1204; in exchange for a payment of 500 marks each, both were allowed to retain their Norman estates for a year and a day. If they wanted to retain them beyond that, they would have to do homage to Philip as Normandy's new ruler. To all the other Anglo-Norman barons, whose estates had simply been seized during the conquest, the French king gave the same ultimatum: do homage within twelve months, or lose your lands forever.[12]

Some of the barons apparently nurtured the hope that there might be a peaceful solution to their dilemma – a diplomatic formula that would enable them to recognize Philip as their lord in Normandy and John as their lord in England. According to the so-called 'Anonymous of Béthune', a chronicler with close links to the English court, a group of barons approached John soon after the fall of Normandy with just such a proposal, assuring the king that their hearts would still be with him, even if they did homage to Philip with their bodies. John, in response, said he would consider the matter with his counsellors, but unsurprisingly these intimate advisers took a dim view. Baldwin de Béthune, a former household knight who reportedly stood high in the king's esteem, had lost his lands in Normandy to the French as early as 1196. 'Were I in your place,' he said to John, 'if the hearts whose bodies were against me came into my hands, I would throw them down the privy.' At this, says the chronicler, there was much laughter, but the question could not have been answered more decisively: there was to be no more talk of serving two masters. The king was not about to let any of his barons pledge allegiance to a man who had deprived him of his patrimony. If they wanted to recover their lost lands, their only option was to join him in fighting for them.[13]

John faced another major problem besides the lukewarm support of his baronage. Mounting a war on the scale required to reverse the defeats of 1203–4 would require massive resources – not only equipment such as ships, siege engines, crossbow bolts and carts, but also mercenaries, sailors and horses, plus the vast quantities of food, drink and other supplies they would need whilst on campaign. It was an almost endless list, all of which ultimately boiled down to one thing: money. Knights might fight for free, according to the terms of their service; mercenaries, mariners and merchants ultimately expected to be paid.

In general terms, England's economy in the early thirteenth century was in robust health. A rising population – around 3 million and counting – meant rising prosperity. Growth was visibly strong, with new towns being founded throughout the country at a rapid rate. Indeed, the period between the Norman Conquest and the start of the thirteenth century had witnessed more urban foundation than any other period in English history; John himself would found Liverpool in 1207. Towns old and new were establishing weekly markets, as well as annual fairs, some of which attracted merchants from all over Europe. Travel between these places was becoming easier thanks to greater investment and innovation. More bridges were being built, and in stone rather than wood; horses were replacing oxen for haulage, increasing the speed at which goods could be transported; cartwheels were less likely to break because they were now clad in metal.[14]

The problem in 1204 was inflation. In the decades before John's reign prices had remained fairly stable, but since his accession in 1199 they had rocketed, more than doubling in the space of just five years. One reason for this must have been the run of bad harvests reported in several chronicles, which would have led to increases in the price of food. Another was a perceived drop in the quality of the coinage. England had always prided itself on its silver pennies, the weight and fineness of which had been fixed soon after the Norman Conquest (giving us the word sterling, from the Old English *steor*, meaning 'fixed'). But in John's reign the weight had become noticeably varied; in government documents we see references to both 'strong pennies' and 'weak pennies'. The official line, picked up by the chroniclers, was to blame criminals, who were shaving small amounts of silver off the king's coinage. So-called 'coin-clipping' was always a problem in the Middle Ages, and no doubt at a time when prices were already rising, more people were tempted to make their money go further by such methods. But what is true of individuals is also true of institutions, and it is impossible to dispel entirely the notion that John's government may for a time have encouraged its moneyers to mint underweight coins as a quick and easy way to get more money. Whatever the true cause, once people noticed the drop in quality, it would have made a bad situation much worse. Sellers would either have refused 'weak' pennies, or else demanded more of them, pushing up prices further. People who had been hoarding money, seeing the value of their savings plummet, would have tried to offload them quickly, increasing the amount of coin in circulation and contributing further still to the upward inflationary trend. Confidence in the coinage was in danger of collapse.

By the autumn of 1204 the situation had become so acute that John and his ministers felt compelled to act, and initiated a nationwide reform. The Crown normally recalled and reissued all the coin in circulation every generation or so, though usually with the aim of turning a profit. The only precedent for restoring confidence had been Henry I's brutal re-coinage of 1124, in which the king ordered not only the complete replacement of his currency, but the mutilation of all his moneyers, each of whom was condemned to lose his right hand and genitals. John's measures in 1204 were not nearly so draconian. On 9 November he simply announced that no one was to have substandard coins after 13 January the following year; anyone found in possession of such money after that date would have it bored through and confiscated for the king's own use. There is a strong possibility, in fact, that John's measures were not harsh enough. Although new, heavier coins began to be minted at the beginning of 1205, old ones were allowed to remain in circulation so long as they were no more than one-eighth lighter than the new standard. As a result it is possible that no more than half of the currency was actually replaced. The upheaval and unpopularity of a full re-coinage was thus avoided, but whether John's reform would be enough to restore confidence in sterling and stop the country's runaway inflation remained to be seen.[15]

By the start of 1205 John's woes were increasing. As Ralph of Coggeshall explains, all of England was disturbed at this point by the rumour that a French invasion was imminent. Philip Augustus was still attracting lots of new men to his banner, especially 'those who had lost great incomes in England'. During the previous autumn, John had seized the English estates of those barons who had chosen to remain in Normandy and pledge their allegiance to the French king. This was an entirely reasonable retaliatory move, and had given John a massive windfall of lands (the so-called 'Lands of the Normans') which he was able to use to reward his loyal followers. At the same time, however, it created an equally cold logic for the Normans themselves. In order to regain their lost English lands, their only hope was to join Philip in his projected conquest.[16]

Fearing this invasion, John summoned a council to London for the middle of January, and overhauled the country's security arrangements. It was already the case that all able-bodied men were expected to turn out in the kingdom's defence, but John now introduced ferocious new penalties for those who failed to do so: landed men were threatened with perpetual disinheritance, while landless ones were promised permanent servitude. The king also appointed new constables to every shire, and beneath them in every city and sub-district, whose job it would be to muster local forces 'against foreigners, or against any other disturbers of the peace'. As this telling line suggests, John feared internal subversion as much as French invasion. If Philip Augustus succeeded in landing troops in England and started winning territory, even those barons who had remained in England might decide to switch sides in the hope of regaining their Norman estates. Such fears may have haunted John for some time: according to Ralph of Coggeshall, the king had failed to raise an army in England in 1204 because he had 'suspicions of treachery among some of his men'. All those who attended the January council, therefore – earls, barons, bishops and abbots – were required to take an oath of loyalty, which was afterwards administered throughout the whole kingdom to every male over the age of twelve. Such oaths had been used by previous kings during times of crisis.[17]

Whom among his magnates did John suspect? One man who certainly came under a cloud at this moment was Ranulf, earl of Chester. Ranulf, born in 1170, was a similar age to the king, and may indeed have grown up alongside him, since as a teenager he had been a ward at the court of Henry II. But despite (or perhaps because of) such youthful proximity, the two men had apparently never seen eye to eye. Ranulf had been one of the greatest landowners in Normandy, and hence one of the greatest losers from the French conquest. But, unlike other magnates such as William Marshal, he had received no subsequent grants of compensation from the Lands of the Normans, nor any new lands at the time of John's accession – not even those he considered to be his by hereditary right. John, for his part, seems to have regarded Ranulf with suspicion because of his family connections. The earl had twice been married into the Breton nobility, and in the spring of 1203 his second wife's family had defected to Philip Augustus – a move that had prompted John to seize Ranulf's estates. That seizure was only temporary, and the earl soon satisfied John of his own good faith. But in the winter of 1204–5, he fell under suspicion for a second time. On 14 December the king again ordered that Ranulf's estates be confiscated, asserting on this occasion that the earl had allied himself to the Welsh.[18]

As before, Ranulf moved quickly to quell John's fears. He was back at court by the time of the January council and so presumably took the oath of loyalty: before the end of the month some of his confiscated lands had been restored.[19] But there is reason to think that in general this council was not a success, and that other magnates may have avoided taking the oath by failing to attend. One man who was almost certainly absent was Roger de Montbegon, for his lands, like those of Ranulf of Chester, had also been seized in December. Roger was also a northerner; his main castle was at Hornby in Lancashire, and his other estates were spread across Yorkshire, Nottinghamshire and Lincolnshire. Although he and Ranulf are the only two men named in the king's writ that December, they are unlikely to have been the only ones who fell under suspicion. If disaffection during John's reign had a geographical focus, it was the north.

The north of England, viewed from Westminster or Winchester, was a far-off place where they did things differently. As well as being geographically distant, it was also hard to reach, cut off by the wide estuary of the River Humber and the bogs of Yorkshire and Cheshire. It was culturally distinct, too, a legacy of extensive Viking settlement during the ninth and tenth centuries, and for the same reason it had remained to a large extent politically separate until the Norman Conquest.[20] Since then the Normans and afterwards the Angevins had done their best to counteract these tendencies by imposing their will on the north, but not without provoking political discontent. John himself had visited the north many times, making four separate trips in the first five years of his reign, and on each occasion extracting large sums of money. During his visit of 1201, for example, he fined the citizens of York £100 for failing to welcome him with sufficient honour, and (according to the northern chronicler Roger of Howden) had even gone digging for buried treasure at Corbridge – without success.[21]

Royal demands for money seem to have lain at the root of northern disaffection during the winter of 1204–5. Since the Norman Conquest, all those who held their lands directly from the king had been obliged to supply him with military service. If for some reason (illness, for example) they failed to do so, they had to make a payment instead called scutage (or 'shield money', from *scutum*, shield). Although it generated usefully large sums for the Crown, scutage had not been particularly onerous during the reigns of John's predecessors. Henry II had demanded it on only eight occasions in the course of his thirty-five-year reign, and Richard only four times during his decade in power. John, by

contrast, had already demanded five scutages by the end of 1204
– one in every year apart from 1200. He had also levied it at a
higher rate than his predecessors, and ahead of campaigns rather
than afterwards. In 1204 he had collected scutage even though
there had been no campaign at all that year. John had also adopted
Richard's one-off experiment of imposing additional fines for
the privilege of paying scutage, and made them a matter of routine,
demanding heavy fines for every one of his five levies.[22]

John's awareness of growing discontent in the north is reflected
in his expenditure during the latter half of 1204: castles were
repaired at York, Tickhill and Carlisle, and their garrisons reinforced by additional crossbowmen. Then, in February 1205, in
the wake of his less than satisfactory January council, the king
himself set out for the north, despite the fact that England was
experiencing one of the worst winters anyone could remember.
(It was so cold, wrote Ralph of Coggeshall, that the Thames could
be crossed on foot, and the frozen ground could not be ploughed.)
For three days in early March John held court in York. On
6 March he showed favour to Ranulf of Chester, who had followed
him north, granting the earl the lands he claimed by marriage
in Yorkshire, and also pardoning some of his debts. Around the
same time, the king settled matters with Roger de Montbegon,
though in this case the treatment was more stick than carrot.
Roger received back his confiscated lands, but it was noted that
his castle at Hornby was being restored 'for as long as he serves
the king well and faithfully', and that, in order to guarantee this
good behaviour, Roger had been required to hand over four
hostages.[23]

John returned south in time for a new great council which
assembled in Oxford towards the end of March. This must have
been summoned soon after the previous council had broken up,
and in itself suggests that the earlier meeting had not gone as
well as hoped. Now, in the wake of the king's visit to the north,
there appears to have been greater consensus. All the earls and
barons present swore that 'they would render him due obedience'.[24]

But this consensus came at the cost of political concessions. In the first place, John dropped his demand for scutage from three northern counties (Yorkshire, Lincolnshire and Northumberland). Secondly, and more notably, the king was obliged to swear an oath of his own. According to one chronicler, the magnates compelled John to promise 'that he would, by their counsel, maintain the rights of the kingdom inviolate, to the utmost of his power'. These brief words are laden with significance. John's barons had complained about their rights once or twice in the past, but the phrase 'rights of the kingdom' suggests that, on this occasion at least, they were demanding something more than simply the redress of their private grievances. Equally significant and novel is the magnates' demand that John should maintain those rights 'by their counsel'. The feeling among the baronage was clearly that the king was not listening to their advice, and was far too reliant on his intimate advisers – the foreigners who shared his desire to mount a reconquest in France. In return for their 'due obedience', the barons wanted a greater say in royal government.[25]

The re-establishment of political consensus came not a minute too soon, for French invasion plans had in the meantime been gathering pace. In February Philip Augustus had patched up a quarrel between two of his vassals, the count of Boulogne and the duke of Brabant, and persuaded them to spearhead an attack on England, promising that he would follow within a month of their landing. As soon the Oxford council was over, John moved south to Winchester and issued writs of military summons. It had been decided, the king explained, 'with the assent of the arch-bishops, bishops, earls, barons, and all our faithful men of England', to assemble a select force: one knight in every ten was to muster in London on 1 May, fully armed and equipped, 'prepared to go in our service wherever we should bid them, and to remain in our service in defence of our realm for as long as necessary'.[26]

John had in fact already decided that the best form of defence was attack. His plan was to mount a continental campaign of the kind that had failed to launch the previous year due to lack of magnate support. This time he began to assemble two separate forces on the south coast: a main one at Portsmouth, where a decade earlier Richard I had established a royal naval base, and a supplementary force at Dartmouth, to be captained by his bastard son, Geoffrey (who steps unheralded on to the stage at this moment). Most chroniclers believed, probably correctly, that the object of these military preparations was Poitou, and that the king's plan was to attack Philip Augustus from the south. It is just possible, however, that John intended a two-pronged attack, and that the Portsmouth force was intended for Normandy. Ralph of Coggeshall reports that those French knights who were stationed in Normandy became terrified at the prospect of an English invasion and withdrew from the castles and towns along the coast.

Throughout April and into May, John concentrated all his energy and resources into equipping these two forces. At every major port in southern England, and in Ireland too, the fleet of galleys built by his brother – reduced in number from seventy to fifty as a result of its disastrous attempt to relieve the Isle of Andely – was repaired and refitted, at a total cost of almost £1,000. Hundreds of other ships were seized, in some cases as early as February, and pressed into royal service. Thousands of sailors were assembled at Portsmouth, and vast quantities of bacon and venison were carted there to feed them, along with all manner of military paraphernalia: defensive hurdles, crossbow bolts, nails for horseshoes. 'Oh what a huge sum of money, what piles of supplies, what endless costs were incurred,' said Ralph of Coggeshall, 'making ready and getting together the ships, stockpiling the foodstuffs and the weapons of war.'[27]

At some point soon into these preparations, John postponed the muster of his land forces, and moved it from London to Northampton. Crossbowmen from castles all over England had been ordered there in their hundreds. Prisoners had been pardoned, officially as a pious act for the soul of the king's dear departed mother, in reality to swell the amount of available manpower. John himself arrived in Northampton on 21 May and five days later marched his host south to meet the fleet at Portsmouth. The quaysides must have been crammed with sailors, the Solent filled with ships. One chronicler, Gervase of Canterbury, prosaically reports that the fleet contained 1,500 vessels. 'They say that never had so many ships sailed into any English port to cross the Channel,' wrote Ralph of Coggeshall, 'and that never had such a large army of stalwart knights been assembled in England, all of whom were keen and eager to go on expedition with the king.'[28]

It was around this point, however, that John received some scandalous news about the man who was supposed to be the most stalwart knight of all. William Marshal, knowing that his year and a day was almost up, had quietly crossed the Channel and done homage to Philip Augustus for his lands in Normandy. Soon afterwards he appeared before John in person and a tremendous row ensued. It is described at length in *The History of William Marshal*, which tries its utmost to justify an act that obviously did great damage to its hero's reputation. According to the *History*, the Marshal had been sent to France on a secret peace mission by John himself, and had obtained the king's prior permission to do homage to Philip, only to find on his return that the king denied all of this. ('"By God," said the king, "I did nothing of the sort!"') It is a wholly unconvincing story, undermined by numerous errors, not least the author's attempt to pretend that Normandy was not yet fully conquered. Despite the *History*'s claims to the contrary, John had good reason to be furious.[29]

While he was waiting at Portsmouth harbour, says the *History*, the king decided to revisit the issue. Surrounded by his other barons, he sat down facing the sea, and summoned the Marshal before him to account for his behaviour. Again the earl insisted he had only been acting on John's orders, and again the king denied it. John then put the issue to the test. 'Here's what I want,' he said to the Marshal. 'You will come with me to Poitou, without delay, to fight the king of France, the man to whom you've done homage, to regain my inheritance.' When the Marshal replied that he could not do so, the king again became very angry, and demanded that the other barons present pass judgement on the earl. The barons, however, balked at this demand. 'By God's teeth!'

swore John, 'I can well see that none of my barons is with me in this matter … I shall have to consult with my bachelors,' and so saying, he led his household knights away to consult in private. They agreed that the Marshal's behaviour was inexcusable, but none of them was willing to take on the great warrior in a judicial duel. Seeing that neither his barons nor his bachelors was willing to give him the judgement he wanted, the king got up and went to dinner.[30]

Deeply irritating though it was, the situation with the Marshal did not deflect John from his wider purpose. Preparations for the great expedition continued. The assembled ships were shared out among the various nobles and loaded with food and weapons. But, as the day of departure approached, the Marshal again came before the king, accompanied by the archbishop of Canterbury, and this time told him to call the expedition off. The whole plan, they argued, was dangerous and misconceived. The French king's forces were more numerous than their own; they had no safe refuge overseas, and John's allies in Poitou were not to be trusted. Moreover, if the king and all his knights left England, the country would be exposed to exactly the kind of invasion they knew was being planned, and 'seeking to recover the land that had been lost, he would lose what he still had'. Such a risky military adventure, they further pointed out, was all the more hazardous in that John had no obvious heir – no surviving brothers, and as yet no legitimate children.[31]

It is clear that this opposition amounted to more than the Marshal. The archbishop of Canterbury, Hubert Walter, was not some hand-wringing pacifist, worried about the human cost of war, but a man of vast governmental and military experience. A creature of King Richard, Hubert had accompanied the Lionheart on crusade and fought with distinction in many battles. He had acted as Richard's chief minister, and was currently serving as John's chancellor. He was, in short, a lynchpin of royal government, an elder statesman who commanded the respect not only of the clergy but the baronage too. He and the Marshal had clearly not approached the king as isolated critics, but as representatives of the whole political class. The barons evidently believed that, when they had sworn to help John defend the kingdom, this did not amount to a pledge to follow him as far as Poitou. As *The History of William Marshal* says, 'many were displeased at the prospect'. The scale of the opposition is evident from the fact that the king was all but physically overpowered. John, says Ralph of Coggeshall, was not persuaded by their arguments, and not deterred until the Marshal and the archbishop declared that 'they would detain him violently, lest the whole kingdom be brought into confusion by his departure'.[32]

And that seems to be essentially what happened. Around 10 June, the king sailed from Portsmouth to Winchester, 'unwillingly' according to Gervase of Canterbury, 'weeping and wailing' in the words of Coggeshall. 'Overcome by the pressure of his advisers', he finally assented to their demands. A token force of knights and nobles would be sent to assist the king's Poitevin subjects, but John himself would remain in England, and the rest of the great fleet and army – assembled for so long, and at such great cost – would be disbanded. The troops themselves, especially the sailors, says Coggeshall, giving us a rare insight into opinion below the ranks of the baronage, thought it an abominable decision, and left cursing the archbishop and the king's other counsellors.[33]

Even then, John was not prepared to abandon his plan. After two days at Winchester he gave his advisers the slip and returned to Portsmouth, where he went on board ship with his own followers and put to sea. A rumour ran around the country that he had crossed the Channel, says Coggeshall, but in fact John had gone no further than the Isle of Wight. By this stage even his intimates were urging him to stay at home. And so, after sailing about aimlessly for a further two days, the king finally put in to Studland Bay in Dorset, his plans for reconquest once again defeated.[34]

4

A Pact From Hell

1189–1194

Henry II died on 6 July 1189 in his castle at Chinon, and from there his body was carried along the Loire to Fontevraud, where it was laid in the abbey church. A short time later his rebellious son Richard arrived, accompanied, in all probability, by his younger brother John, who had lately defected to Richard's camp. John's defection had undoubtedly been a heavy blow to Henry, possibly (as several chroniclers opined) the blow that finally killed him. It should, however, be remembered that the principal cause of the king's suffering during the final years of his life had been his long-running feud with Richard. According to two chroniclers, as Richard drew near to his father's corpse, blood flowed from the nose of the dead king, 'as if', said Roger of Howden, 'his spirit were angered by his approach'. If this was a scene familiar from Arthurian romances, it nevertheless indicated that some people held Richard responsible for Henry's death. Howden and others describe Richard as full of contrition at Fontevraud, weeping bitterly. *The History of William Marshal*, by contrast, claims he showed no emotion, standing silently at the head of the bier for a while, before turning to his servants, saying, 'Bury richly the king my father.'[1]

Despite the years of uncertainty caused by Henry's refusal to name his successor, there was no question about what would happen next. Richard had vindicated his right to his inheritance by force of arms, and now succeeded unopposed to all his father's possessions. At Fontevraud he made peace with the men who had stood loyally by Henry to the last, and then rode north to Normandy, where he was invested as duke on 20 July in Rouen Cathedral. Two days later he travelled to Gisors on the border with France to meet with Philip Augustus. The French king, lately his ally, automatically became a rival as Richard stepped into his father's shoes. In spite of this, and by postponing contentious issues (such as the Vexin), an accord was quickly reached. In return for a sizeable payment of 24,000 marks, Philip returned almost all the territories he had recently conquered with Richard's assistance, and recognized him as heir to all the Plantagenet dominions. Their conference over, Richard rode to Barfleur and sailed for England, where his mother, already released from her long captivity, was preparing for his coronation.[2]

What role would John play in this new regime? On the one hand he was clearly very important. Richard, still unmarried, lacked legitimate children; John, his only surviving brother, was his most obvious heir. As such John needed to be accommodated, and accorded appropriate wealth and status. Before his death Henry II had apparently granted him lands in both England and Normandy, and Richard proved willing to honour this bequest. Soon after his investiture as duke, he gave John the county of Mortain in western Normandy, and promised him £4,000 of land in England.[3]

On the other hand, Richard clearly did not trust his younger brother. That there was no great love lost between them might be implied by the manner of their crossing to England. Not only did they set sail from Barfleur in different ships (which could be viewed as nothing other than prudent), they also put into different English ports, Richard landing at Portsmouth to the jubilant reception laid on by his mother, while John disembarked at Dover without any recorded fanfare.[4]

More suggestive still of the suspicion that John continued to provoke was his sudden marriage. The match Henry II had originally brokered in 1173, by which John would have married the daughter of the count of Savoy, had come to nothing – within a year of the agreement the girl was dead. But in 1176 Henry had found his youngest son a fresh marital prospect in the form of Isabella, the eldest daughter of the earl of Gloucester. This was principally a means of increasing John's landed estate, and on the earl's death in 1183 the old king had duly seized his lands for John's future use. No marriage, however, had followed. By this point Henry was reviewing his options, having recently lost his eldest son and fallen out with his second. By the end of the same year, he had been openly floating the idea that John rather than Richard might be married to Philip Augustus' sister, Alice. As his sons died off, and the feud with Richard intensified, Henry had every reason for wanting to keep John's matrimonial options open.[5]

Richard, once he was in charge, wanted to shut them down. Within days of the brothers' return to England in 1189 John was married to Isabella, his long-term fiancée: their wedding took place at John's castle at Marlborough on 29 August. To be fair, John's thoughts on the matter are unknown; it may be that he accepted his bride with alacrity. Isabella, sadly, is a completely anonymous character, whose attractions apart from her extensive lands are unrecorded. She was, however, already around thirty years old in 1189, and thus likely to have been regarded as something of an old maid by her twenty-two-year-old groom. Later events certainly suggest that theirs was not a match made in heaven.[6]

The notion that John was married at Richard's insistence is reinforced by the similar treatment of their half-brother, Geoffrey, the most prominent of Henry II's several bastard children. Born around 1151 and raised honourably in the royal household, Geoffrey had been marked out for advancement in the Church, yet had shown a notable reluctance to commit to a clerical career. Elected as bishop of Lincoln in 1173, he eventually resigned the position rather than take holy orders. In September 1189 Richard compelled him to do so, appointing him as archbishop of York, despite the objections of the cathedral chapter and of Geoffrey himself. By forcing him into a tonsure, Richard ended any misplaced hopes his half-brother may have entertained with regard to the succession.[7]

The reason Richard was so keen to keep his brothers' ambitions in check was simple: he was determined to depart on crusade. After the fall of Jerusalem to Muslim forces in 1187, the Christian communities of the Holy Land had been reduced to a handful of coastal cities and isolated inland castles. The pressure on western princes to come to their rescue remained intense, and Richard, having taken the cross almost two years earlier, was anxious to waste no more time. On 3 September 1189 he was crowned in Westminster Abbey, and invested with all the powers and responsibilities of kingship. John played a part in the proceedings by carrying one of the ceremonial swords. Two weeks later, the new king held the first great council of his reign at Pipewell Abbey in Northamptonshire, and set about delegating those same powers and responsibilities to others, setting out the details of his regency scheme. In his absence England was to be ruled by two justiciars, the earl of Essex and the bishop of Durham, with the help of a number of less distinguished but more administratively experienced assistants. John, who might have expected some role in the running of government, however nominal, was not included.[8]

For three more months Richard busied himself in England, raising money for his expedition and attending to the kingdom's security. From Pipewell he went west to Worcester to make peace with the various rulers of Wales. (John, sent to besiege the castle at Carmarthen, made a separate deal that Richard refused to ratify.) In December he travelled to Canterbury to receive the king of Scots, William the Lion, and, in return for a generous payment, tore up the humiliating peace treaty that Henry II had imposed on William after his capture in 1174. From Canterbury Richard went directly to Dover and crossed the Channel, to begin making similar preparations for departure in his continental territories.[9]

Before leaving England, Richard had honoured his earlier promise to John by making him a massive grant of land. John had already received a lot of land soon after the coronation – most notably the earldom of Gloucester brought to him by his marriage to Isabella, but also seven other substantial lordships (Ludgershall, Marlborough, Peveril, Tickhill, Eye, Lancaster and Wallingford), as well as other manors and the profits of two royal forests. Together these estates brought John around £1,170 a year, a sizeable sum, but one which fell a long way short of the £4,000 he had been promised. At Canterbury Richard had therefore granted his younger brother six whole counties, namely Nottinghamshire, Derbyshire, Somerset, Dorset, Devon and Cornwall – a huge amount of territory, concentrated in the Midlands and the south-west, which brought his income comfortably above the required amount.

Some people subsequently criticized Richard for this grant. William of Newburgh commented that John seemed to have been given almost a third of England, and condemned Richard for his 'immoderate and improvident liberality'. Newburgh, however (like later historians who echoed his criticisms) wrote with the knowledge of how the story would end. A more charitable interpretation of Richard's actions would allow that he was simply fulfilling Henry II's last wishes. Moreover, the new king, in giving these lands to his younger brother, retained many of the castles within them. (John received the castles at Marlborough, Ludgershall, Peveril and Lancaster, but not, for example, those at Orford, Eye, Wallingford, Tickhill or Gloucester, all of which were reserved to the Crown.) John had been given a lot of land, but not the wherewithal to hold it in a fight.[10]

More legitimate criticism can be levelled at Richard over the person he *did* leave in charge. Around the time of his departure from England, one of his two newly appointed justiciars, the earl of Essex, died, and the king attempted to solve the problem by granting additional powers to his chancellor, William Longchamp. A clerk who had been in Richard's service for some time, Longchamp was clearly a man whose abilities the king held in high regard. Formerly the chancellor of Poitou, he had been promoted to the same position in England at the time of Richard's coronation, and elevated to become bishop of Ely a short time later. Longchamp's origins, however, were comparatively humble – he was a scion of a modest knightly family – and so his rapid rise inevitably excited envy and disapproval. According to the chronicler Richard of Devizes, who wrote a wonderfully opinionated account of these years, the new chancellor was 'a remarkable person, who made up for the shortness of his stature by his arrogance, counting on his lord's affection and presuming on his goodwill'.[11]

Whether his faults were real or maliciously invented, Longchamp plainly did not see eye to eye with the surviving justiciar, Hugh du Puiset, the bishop of Durham. By February reports of their malfunctioning relationship must have reached Richard in distant Aquitaine, for at that point he summoned both men to attend a council. When it convened in Normandy the following month the king announced that henceforth Longchamp, as well as continuing as chancellor, would be England's new *chief* justiciar; the bishop of Durham would be responsible only for those lands north of the Humber.

Also present in the same meeting at Richard's command were John and his half-brother Geoffrey. There is nothing to suggest that either had played any part in the disputes between the king's regents, but Richard revealed his growing distrust of the pair by taking an additional security measure, and making both of them swear to stay out of England for the next three years. In John's case, however, this provision was immediately diluted thanks to the intervention of Eleanor of Aquitaine. At their mother's request, Richard allowed that John could enter and leave England provided he had Longchamp's permission.[12]

Whether or not John returned to England after this meeting is unclear – his movements in 1190 are for the most part mysterious. But Longchamp recrossed the Channel at once and took immediate steps to tighten his grip on power. He began by orchestrating the downfall of the bishop of Durham, interfering in his jurisdiction north of the Humber and arresting him when he came to complain. The bishop protested to the king and regained his liberty, but not his office; in June Richard confirmed that Longchamp would have authority over the whole kingdom. In the meantime the chief justiciar had been further increasing his control by appointing his own men as sheriffs and as keepers of royal castles – replacing, in some cases, men who had paid handsomely to have these offices only the previous year. He also invested large sums improving the defences of key fortresses; almost £3,000 was spent on the Tower of London alone. Nor was it just in the secular sphere that Longchamp's pervasive influence was felt. At Richard's request the pope made him a papal legate, giving him unrivalled authority over the English Church. As top ecclesiastical positions fell vacant, they were similarly filled by the justiciar's friends and relatives. 'The laity at that time felt him to be a king, and more than a king,' wrote William of Newburgh, 'the clergy a pope and more than a pope. Indeed, both of them [felt him to be] an intolerable tyrant.'[13]

No one can have felt more aggrieved at Longchamp's overbearing behaviour than the king's younger brother. Apart from the fact that a low-born cleric had been left to determine whether he – an Angevin prince – should be allowed to enter or leave the kingdom, John must have perceived the justiciar's actions as a programme intended to keep him in his place. He had deliberately been left with only a few castles, but Longchamp contrived to make it fewer still, confiscating the castles of Bolsover and the Peak in Derbyshire. Moreover, the royal castles that the justiciar had chosen to repair and refortify were all located near to John's lands or those of his associates, as if in expectation of trouble. His associates were also marked out for special attention. His seneschal, John Marshal (brother of the more famous William), lost his job as sheriff of York and keeper of York Castle to Longchamp's own brother, Osbert. And William Marshal himself (who was closely aligned with John at this point, despite his biographer's later attempts to disguise it) also clashed with the justiciar, who for a time tried to deprive him of Gloucester Castle, even to the extent of laying siege to it.[14]

Complaints about Longchamp's behaviour were naturally sent

to Richard, but the king was becoming increasingly hard to reach. He and Philip Augustus had finally set out on their journey to the east in July 1190; in August they then sailed, independently, along the west coast of Italy, and by September both had arrived in Sicily. Richard's reception in Sicily, however, was a hostile one, and his men clashed violently with the locals. In the process of resolving this conflict, the king made an extraordinary decision – one which had major repercussions for politics in England.[15]

Had Richard arrived in Sicily twelve months earlier, he would have received a much warmer welcome, for back then his sister Joan had been married to the island's ruler, King William II. But William had died in November 1189, and the Sicilian crown had passed to his illegitimate cousin, Tancred of Lecce. Tancred's hold on power was tenuous and he had treated Joan with suspicion, withholding her widow's dower and keeping her in close confinement. This obviously did not bode well for good relations with Richard. According to Roger of Howden, an eyewitness, the English king sailed into Messina that September 'in such magnificence and to such a noise of trumpets and clarions that a tremor ran though all who were in the city'. This demonstration of power had some effect on Tancred, to the extent that he released Joan from captivity and delivered her to her brother's camp. But in the meantime the crusading army had begun fighting with the population of Messina, many of whom were Greek, and some of whom were Muslim. When a riot broke out in early October, Richard responded by taking the city by force. As an added security measure, he built a wooden castle on a nearby hill, to which he gave the unsubtle name of Mategriffon, or 'Kill the Greeks'.[16]

Tancred had no option but to negotiate with his unwelcome visitors. In return for peace he agreed to pay Richard 40,000 ounces of gold – half to compensate Joan for her lack of dower, and half in lieu of the ships and supplies his predecessor had promised to contribute to the crusade. As was common in such cases, the deal was to be sealed by a royal wedding. Richard, alas, had no legitimate sons for such purposes, but he did have a three-year-old nephew. The boy, named Arthur, was the only son of his late brother, Geoffrey. He had not been born at the time of Geoffrey's death in the summer of 1186 – indeed, he must have only just been conceived, for he did not make his appearance until 29 March the following year. Young Arthur was the obvious, not to say the only solution to his uncle's diplomatic needs, and it was duly agreed that he would marry one of Tancred's three daughters. At the same moment, Richard also announced that, in the event he should die with no sons of his own, Arthur would be his heir.[17]

This, to put it mildly, was explosive. Although everyone was aware of Arthur's existence in the autumn of 1190, he was as yet only a small child, who might not make it beyond the hazardous years of infancy. Richard, moreover, had done nothing thus far to discourage the notion that his successor, in default of any sons, would be his younger brother, John. On the contrary, he had done much to encourage it by his generous provision for John in England, and there is even evidence to suggest that, during their meeting in March 1190, he had named John as his default successor in Normandy. John, said William of Newburgh, 'expected to become the successor to the kingdom, should the king, perchance, not survive his laborious and perilous undertaking'.[18]

Quite what Richard hoped to achieve, therefore, by suddenly naming Arthur as his heir is a mystery. Possibly his only intention was to make his nephew a more attractive bridegroom in order to extract maximum advantage from Tancred. According to Newburgh, the news of Arthur's nomination was kept secret, and the only person informed in England was the justiciar, William Longchamp. But Longchamp, continues Newburgh, passed the message on to the king of Scots, hoping to secure his support for Arthur's claim if the need arose, and no doubt he did the same with others. Somehow, early in the new year 1191, the cat was let out of the bag, and John found out.[19]

At first, says Newburgh, he hid his indignation, but began secretly building up his own party of supporters. Presumably by this point, if not before, he had returned to England. As the tension mounted, a meeting between the two sides was arranged at Winchester on 24 March. According to Richard of Devizes, our only informant, the debate concerned 'the custody of certain castles, and the money granted to the count [of Mortain, i.e. John] by his brother at the Exchequer'. This makes it sound as if John had not received all the money he felt was his due, and was belatedly contesting the extent to which Longchamp had gained control of the most important royal castles. In any succession dispute, these fortresses would be crucial; they were, in William of Newburgh's well-turned phrase, 'the bones of the kingdom'. Whatever was said at Winchester, however, failed to defuse the situation. As Easter came and went, it was obvious that men were preparing for civil war. 'Certain nobles became busy', says Devizes. 'Castles were strengthened, towns were fortified, ditches were dug.' Letters were sent in secret, soliciting the support of powerful people against the justiciar. Meanwhile John was travelling about the country with a large following, and 'he did not prohibit or restrain his followers from calling him the king's heir'.[20]

At last, says Devizes, 'the lid came off the pot'. Shortly before midsummer (21 June), Longchamp demanded that the keeper of the royal castle at Lincoln, Gerard de Camville, surrender its custody and swear allegiance to him as regent. Camville, whose right to hold the castle had only recently been confirmed by Richard, refused the order and went instead to swear allegiance to John. On learning of this open defiance, the justiciar sent overseas for foreign mercenaries, and in the meantime took such troops as he could raise to lay siege to Lincoln. John in turn rose to defend Camville's right. Moving north, he quickly forced the surrender of the ill-prepared royal castles at nearby Tickhill and Nottingham, and he sent messengers to Longchamp, explaining (in the evocative words of Roger of Howden) that he would 'visit him with a rod of iron' if Camville was not immediately reinstated.[21]

At this moment, with England apparently on the brink of civil war, an emissary arrived from Richard. Walter of Coutances, archbishop of Rouen but an Englishman by birth, had followed the king as far as Sicily, but had been sent home in April, Richard having finally realized he needed to do something about Longchamp's growing unpopularity. He arrived in southern England on 27 June and hastened north to act as intermediary between the two hostile factions. Negotiations were evidently not easy. The justiciar, says Richard of Devizes, demanded that John give up the castles he had seized and stand trial for having broken his oath to stay out of the kingdom. John, on being told this, 'became unrecognizable in all his body. Wrath cut furrows across his forehead; his burning eyes shot sparks; rage darkened the ruddy colour of his face.' At length, however, both sides agreed to a day of mediation, which was fixed for 28 July at Winchester. Longchamp in the meantime raised the siege of Lincoln and returned to London.[22]

The chances of a peaceful settlement at Winchester must have seemed bleak. Both sides appealed to their supporters to turn out fully armed, and both sides had taken the additional precaution of raising troops from Wales. (John kept his concealed near the conference place, which was outside the city walls.) Nevertheless, a peace agreement was reached, the terms of which have survived. For the most part they favoured John. He agreed to give up Nottingham and Tickhill castles, but the men named as their new keepers were members of his affinity. He promised not to harbour outlaws in his lands, but this merely serves to highlight how independent his power had become. Meanwhile his supporter Gerard de Camville was reinstated as keeper of Lincoln Castle, and all new fortifications raised since Richard's departure were to be dismantled. Richard's absence, and the possibility he might not return, linger over the whole document; John was clearly trying to strengthen his hand against such an outcome. In this respect, he won a crucial point, not mentioned in the treaty, but emphasized by both Devizes and Newburgh. Longchamp also agreed to drop his support for Arthur, and to support John's right to the throne in the event of Richard's death.[23]

Good as it was for John, the deal achieved at Winchester had no clear winner. Whatever concessions had been wrung from the justiciar, he still remained in power, and he still had Richard's support: according to Richard of Devizes, the archbishop of Rouen had returned with the particular message from the king that his brother was to obey Longchamp.[24]

What upset the fragile peace in England was the return of John and Richard's half-brother Geoffrey. The archbishop-elect of York had finally had his consecration approved by the pope in May, and the ceremony took place in Tours in August. Possessed of his new authority, Geoffrey decided to disregard his oath not to cross the Channel, and asked for John's assistance. John was only too happy to pledge his help, but Longchamp, perceiving the threat to his own authority, gave orders that Geoffrey was to be arrested on sight. Thus when the new archbishop arrived at Dover on 14 September, he was immediately surrounded by soldiers. He managed to escape to the local priory, but after five days the soldiers entered in their mail shirts and dragged him out, banging his head on the pavement. Dressed in his episcopal robes and clinging to his cross, accompanied by a crowd of curious townspeople, Geoffrey was pushed and dragged up the hill to Dover Castle, to be detained at the pleasure of the castellan, who also happened to be Longchamp's brother-in-law.[25]

'The story', says Richard of Devizes, 'went through the country more quickly than the wind.' Geoffrey was seemingly a popular figure among the laity, respected as a soldier and a loyal son; the clergy, whatever they thought of his spiritual deficiencies, objected to his treatment on principle. Inevitably the news that soldiers had violated the sanctuary of a church and injured an archbishop evoked memories of Becket's martyrdom. The outrage was instant. The bishop of Lincoln excommunicated the castellan of Dover, and other bishops added their voices to the outcry. Longchamp, desperately trying to retrieve the situation, ordered Geoffrey's release and gave out that he had never ordered his detention, but to no avail: the country was up in arms.[26]

For John this was the opportunity he had been waiting for. During his earlier clash over Lincoln Castle he had attempted to pose as the champion of those unjustly oppressed by the justiciar's tyranny, claiming that 'he was no longer willing to bear in silence the desolation of his brother's possessions and his realm'. Now he struck up this same tune again with greater gusto. Rushing south from Lancaster to his castle at Marlborough, he sent letters to all the magnates. 'As you love God's honour, and the Church's, and the lord king's, and the realm's, and mine,' he began, 'be at Loddon Bridge on the Saturday next after Michaelmas, between Reading and Windsor, because, God willing, I will meet you there, so that we may deal with certain great and arduous matters concerning the lord king and the realm.'[27]

This meeting, which took place on 5 October, was well attended, with both bishops and barons turning up in large numbers. Longchamp, who had been summoned to account for his actions, advanced heavily armed from London and lurked at nearby Windsor. Walter de Coutances, the archbishop of Rouen and broker of the recent peace, explained to the assembled company how he had lost patience with the justiciar, who had thwarted all his efforts to help govern the realm, as King Richard had commanded. He now produced an additional letter from the king, authorizing him to remove Longchamp from office. The magnates and prelates unanimously agreed that this was the right way forward, and instructed the justiciar to come before them on Monday to hear this judgement.[28]

Longchamp did set out on Monday morning, but then apparently panicked, hearing the news that John was marching on London. In fact all John had done was send his baggage train to London ahead of him, but the justiciar mistook this as an attempt to seize the capital and set out in pursuit. At one point during the journey there was a skirmish between the two households, in the course of which one of John's knights was killed. Longchamp arrived back in London ahead of his rivals and tried to persuade the citizens to bar the gates against them. But the Londoners, stirred up by the recently-arrived Archbishop Geoffrey, refused the justiciar's request, calling him 'a disturber of the land and a traitor', at which point Longchamp and his followers fled to the Tower. When John and the barons arrived later that evening, the citizens came out to welcome them with lanterns and torches.[29]

The following day – Tuesday 8 October – the bells of St Paul's summoned the Londoners and the new arrivals to a second meeting, in which all spoke out against the justiciar. On the authority of the royal letters brought by Walter de Coutances, Longchamp was dismissed from office, and so too were all the friends and relatives he had appointed to positions of power. 'The whole assembly', said Richard of Devizes, 'declared Count John, the king's brother, supreme governor of the whole realm, and ordered that all castles should be turned over to whomever he wanted.' All present, beginning with John himself, renewed their oaths of fealty to Richard, but they also swore to obey John during his brother's absence, and to accept him as king should Richard not return.[30]

Longchamp, still ensconced in the Tower, reportedly fainted when he was told this news the following morning, and had to be revived by having cold water splashed in his face. He stubbornly refused to resign his offices or his castles, telling John's messengers, 'You have forgotten your still-living king.' At length, however, his followers persuaded him to submit to the superior power of his enemies, who had placed the Tower under siege. Thus, on Thursday 10 October, the justiciar emerged to be formally stripped of his offices before a great crowd that had assembled outside the city walls. Courageously, given his predicament, he maintained to the last that he was not resigning his duties, merely being deprived of them by force. After this he was escorted to Dover, one of the three royal castles he was permitted to retain, but shortly afterwards escaped across the Channel. The bishops, earls and barons, meanwhile, wrote a letter to the king, explaining what they had done.[31]

During the summer of 1191, Richard had been winning the victories that would make him a legend. In April he had finally left Sicily with a fleet of 200 ships and perhaps 17,000 men, and in May he had conquered the island of Cyprus. Arriving in the

Holy Land in June, he had captured the city of Acre in July, ending the siege that had begun there two years earlier. In August, after massacring 3,000 Muslim prisoners outside Acre's walls, he had set out further south, and in September he had defeated Saladin's army in battle at Arsuf. On 1 October he sent home a confident newsletter. 'With God's grace,' he wrote, 'we hope to recover the city of Jerusalem and the Holy Sepulchre within twenty days after Christmas, and then return to our own dominions.'[32]

But in the course of making these conquests, the king had fallen out with several of his allies, most notably Philip Augustus. For years Richard had been promising to marry Philip's sister, Alice, but during their stay on Sicily he had at last revealed that this had been a deception. Richard could never consent to marrying Alice, he explained, because she had been his father's mistress – indeed, she had borne Henry II a bastard son. This revelation was forced from Richard because he had made alternative wedding plans. To safeguard Aquitaine during his absence he had entered into an alliance with the king of Navarre, and promised to marry his daughter, Berengaria. She was escorted to Sicily in March by the elderly but indefatigable Eleanor of Aquitaine, and eventually married to Richard in May while the king was still in Cyprus.[33]

Although Richard did his best to placate Philip, paying him 10,000 marks in compensation, the French king had taken the humiliation deeply to heart. He departed from Sicily ahead of the English crusaders and sailed directly to the Holy Land. Once Richard had joined him there, the two of them had done nothing but quarrel, taking different sides in political disputes and arguing over the division of spoils. Eventually, on 22 July, Philip had announced he was leaving for home, claiming he was too ill to continue, and two weeks later he departed. To compound his humiliation, many of his men chose not to accompany him, and remained behind to follow Richard. By October the French king had reached Italy, and by Christmas he was back in France – 'safe and sound', according to Roger of Howden, 'and impudently boasting that he was going to devastate the lands of the king of England'.[34]

Philip's first action, on 20 January 1192, was to meet the seneschal of Normandy on the border with France. Presenting forged documents, he explained that Richard, in rejecting Alice, had relinquished his right to hold the Vexin, and demanded that both his sister and the long-contested territory be handed over. The seneschal and the other barons of Normandy told the French king, in so many words, to get lost, at which point Philip vowed angrily that he would take the Vexin by force. As a first step to making good this threat, he sent an invitation to John, promising to make him ruler of all Richard's continental lands if he would make an honest woman out of Alice.[35]

John, to general consternation, responded enthusiastically to this proposal, and made preparations to sail to France. The fact that he already had a wife was not much of a problem: his marriage to Isabella of Gloucester had been declared invalid by the archbishop of Canterbury immediately after its celebration in 1189 on grounds of consanguinity (both bride and groom were descendants of Henry I). John, presumably at Richard's insistence, had subsequently obtained a provisional dispensation from a visiting papal legate, but since then had not bothered to seek confirmation from the pope. The ties that bound him to Isabella were thus weak, and could easily be undone.[36]

John's eagerness to conspire with Philip Augustus at the start of 1192 is more surprising in view of his apparently strong position the previous autumn. During that period he had been the hero of the hour, a liberator who had delivered the realm from the tyranny of Longchamp, welcomed into London by jubilant crowds. But John's popularity may have been more apparent than real. Richard of Devizes reports that he had been made 'supreme governor of the whole realm' and handed custody of all the royal castles, but if this was ever agreed it had not been subsequently carried through.[37] William of Newburgh states, more credibly, that the magnates had delivered management of the kingdom to the archbishop of Rouen, Walter de Coutances. *The History of William Marshal* adds that the archbishop ruled well and wisely, following the advice of the barons, but shunning the counsels of John, 'since he could see well what John's intentions were'. If this is not entirely true – there is evidence to show that he was consulted on certain issues – there is good reason to think that by the beginning of 1192 John must have been feeling marginalized. He had, of course, been recognized as Richard's heir, should the king die without children of his own. But Richard was now married, and his wife had accompanied him to the Holy Land. Even as John fervently hoped for news of some fatal encounter in the sands of Palestine, he must have feared that the spring would bring letters from his brother announcing the birth of a son.[38]

What prevented John from pushing ahead and accepting Philip's enticing offer was the rapid intervention of his mother. 'Fearing that the light-minded youth might be going to attempt something', says Richard of Devizes, Eleanor of Aquitaine crossed the Channel from Normandy on 11 February. By assuring John that his possessions in England would be confiscated should he leave the kingdom, the former queen and the archbishop of Rouen induced him to stay put. Philip, meanwhile, failed to persuade the nobles of France to participate in his planned invasion of Normandy, there being few things more dishonourable than attacking the lands of an absent crusader.[39]

John was, however, quite capable of causing trouble by himself. Soon after this setback he seized control of two of the most important royal castles, Windsor and Wallingford, somehow convincing their keepers to surrender them and garrisoning them with his own men. The regents responded by summoning a council of magnates to London, intending to bring him to book. But, says Richard of Devizes, 'each one, fearing the count, wanted the question to be put by another mouth rather than by his own'. John's provocative behaviour was highlighting the almost impossible bind in which England's great men found themselves. If they were to uphold Richard's authority they ought not to tolerate its usurpation; but, on the other hand, if Richard died, John would surely become the next king, and punish those who had opposed him.[40]

As if to emphasize their dilemma, while the council was sitting in London news arrived of the return of William Longchamp. The former justiciar had never accepted the legitimacy of his deposition, and during his self-imposed exile he had been busy drumming up support for a comeback. The pope, who naturally objected to the overthrow of a papal legate, had authorized the excommunication of those who had ousted him. Roger of Howden believed that Longchamp had bribed Eleanor of Aquitaine into supporting his readmittance, and William of Newburgh asserted that he had been secretly communicating with John. Whatever the truth, the former justiciar landed at Dover in late March and demanded to be reinstated as the realm's rightful governor.[41]

At this the magnates' attitude towards John was instantly reversed. 'The man whom they had been going to judge a perjurer and an offender against his lord', as Richard of Devizes calls him, was seen as being the only hope of resisting the danger that lurked at Dover. The count himself, meanwhile, was staying at Wallingford Castle, 'laughing at their assemblies', and messengers were sent there to beg him to intervene. After letting them beg for a good long time, he came to London, and allowed himself to be flattered some more by the magnates in council. 'There was no mention of the castles', says Devizes; all the talk was now of removing Longchamp, and John relished the discomfort of his rivals. The former justiciar, he explained, had offered him £700 to remain neutral, and he really needed the money. The regents took the hint and paid him £500 from the Exchequer in return for his continued support, and then sent messengers to Longchamp, informing him of the outcome and commanding him to leave; Longchamp, realizing he had lost the bidding war, returned to the Continent. The whole episode had turned out so well for John it is hard not to suspect he had some hand in orchestrating it. Essentially it was a less dramatic rerun of the events of the previous autumn, John once again delivering the realm from its sometime oppressor, reminding the regents how much they were reliant on his power. In exchange for his services, he exacted more than just money. The council in London concluded its business by again swearing fealty to Richard, and to John as his heir.[42]

Richard had hoped to be back in England by this point, but his plan to be in Jerusalem within twenty days of Christmas 1191 had not come to pass. The crusaders had come close: on Christmas Day itself they were camped just twelve miles from the Holy City, but soon afterwards they were forced to admit that they did not have the manpower or resources to mount an effective siege. In January 1192 they had retired to the coastal town of Ascalon, where they had remained for the next four months.[43]

Soon after Easter (5 April) news reached Richard of the overthrow of William Longchamp the previous autumn; the messenger, presumably sent by Longchamp himself, reported that John was trying to take over the realm, and urged the king to return home. But Richard was undeterred; probably he had also received the reports sent by Walter of Coutances and his fellow regents explaining their reasons for ending the justiciar's regime and assuring him that his affairs were still in good order. In May the king embarked on a fresh military offensive, advancing twenty miles further south to assault the castle of Darum, which succumbed after a four-day siege. At the end of the month, however, a second messenger arrived, informing Richard that his brother was plotting with Philip Augustus. This intelligence, which presumably came from Walter of Coutances, was much more disconcerting, for Philip was capable of doing far greater damage. After agonizing for some time, Richard decided on one final roll of the dice, and agreed to support a second attempt to take Jerusalem. This time he came even closer, and may even have glimpsed the city from afar, but once again he decided in conference with the other crusade leaders that an assault would be impossible. On 4 July the crusading army, paralysed by divisions over strategy, withdrew to the coast and resumed negotiations with Saladin. At the start of September they agreed a truce that would last almost four years – time enough for Richard to settle his urgent affairs in the west. On 9 October the king set sail from the Holy Land, hopeful that before too long he would be able to return.

In the meantime, he had to contend with the problem of how to get home. Philip Augustus had spent the previous twelve months trying to detract from his own humiliation by blackening Richard's name across Europe, accusing him of trickery, treachery and even murder (in April the king-elect of Jerusalem had been killed in mysterious circumstances). As a result there was no obvious safe route for Richard to take. Whatever his plans were, they were dashed by storms that drove his ships into the Italian coast, north-east of Venice. The king and his companions became lost and entered the lands of Duke Leopold of Austria. Leopold, alas, was another crusader who had fallen out with Richard: the king's troops had contemptuously thrown down the duke's banner as they entered Acre, and the insult had prompted Leopold to abandon the crusade. Inevitably Richard's attempt to travel incognito through Austria failed, and he was arrested in a tavern outside Vienna just before Christmas 1192. By the start of the new year, all of Europe had learned that the king of England was a captive.[44]

In England itself the news was greeted for the most part with predictable alarm. Eleanor of Aquitaine was reportedly distressed to hear it; Walter of Coutances wrote of his 'grief of mind' at the misfortune, 'momentous beyond all conception, which has befallen our king'. Others sought to rationalize it as the judgement of God. The dean of St Paul's, Ralph of Diceto, opined Richard's capture was divine retribution for having rebelled against his father.[45]

In John's camp, by contrast, the mood was jubilant. If he had been hoping for Richard's death, captivity was the next best thing. Had not their great-grandfather, Henry I, captured his older brother, Robert Curthose, and kept him in prison for nearly thirty years? John's advisers assured him that the time was ripe to claim the kingdom. Philip Augustus, who had sent the happy news, repeated his offer of the previous year to make John lord of all Richard's lands on the Continent. He rushed to accept, and came out openly in rebellion. 'Setting at naught his fidelity to his brother,' said William of Newburgh, 'he most shamefully declared himself his enemy.'[46]

John now controlled enough royal castles to disregard the regents' earlier threats to dispossess him should he go abroad. Strengthening their garrisons, he hastened across the Channel at the end of January. He met first with the seneschal and barons of Normandy and offered to help them defend the duchy against the expected French attack, provided they accept him as their new lord. When they refused, he rode on to France and entered what Roger of Howden called 'a pact from hell' with Philip Augustus, doing homage to the French king for all Richard's lands, promising to marry Alice and agreeing to surrender the Vexin. In return Philip granted him the county of Artois, a territory he had lately annexed after the death of its previous ruler, the count of Flanders, on crusade. For the first time a king of France had a maritime coast from which to threaten England, and Philip and John now began to do just that, recruiting Flemish mercenaries and assembling an invasion fleet, with the intention of crossing to England at Easter.[47]

Back in England the regents had been busy responding to the crisis and anxiously awaiting news of Richard. By late January they would have known that the king's captor, Duke Leopold, was negotiating to hand him over to his overlord, the Holy Roman Emperor, Henry VI. Henry was another ruler who had been worked on by Philip Augustus after his return from the crusade; as Philip had passed through Italy the two of them had entered a secret alliance. The emperor's eagerness to obtain Richard, however, had less to do with any loyalty to his French ally, and more to do with the sizeable ransom he knew such a high-status prisoner could command. Henry was plagued by rebellion across his wide dominions, and desperately in need of extra funds. The regents in England dispatched two abbots to Germany to discover what his terms would be. In the meantime, they focused on preparing to defend the realm against the feared invasion. An oath of loyalty to Richard was administered across the whole kingdom; coastal towns were strengthened, and troops were raised to guard the shore.[48]

Despite these measures, at some point in the weeks that followed John managed to re-enter the country in secret. He brought with him some Flemish mercenaries and set about trying to rally more support, telling people that his brother was dead. Some believed him, but most remained loyal, including the king of Scots and the various princes of Wales. Having succeeded in raising some Welsh troops, who ravaged the area between Windsor and Kingston, John marched on London and demanded to be given the realm. The Londoners, however, had lately reaffirmed their allegiance to Richard, and together with the regents they rejected his demand. In anger John withdrew to his castles and began attacking his brother's estates.[49]

Now was the supreme test of the loyalty of the magnates, whose predicament had never been so stark. Remaining faithful to Richard would require them to start actively waging war against John, the man who might very easily become their new ruler if Richard failed to return. Shortly before Easter, as they debated what to do, a messenger arrived from the captive king in the shape of Roger of Thurnham, a household knight and former crusader. Thurnham would have been able to tell his audience in London what the two abbots they had sent to Germany were simultaneously hearing from Richard himself: that the king was fit and well, and that negotiations for his release were already in train. If he was privately anxious about John's treachery, he was publicly dismissive, saying, 'My brother John is not the man to seize any land by force, if anyone meets his attack with even the slightest resistance.' Thurnham had arrived in London with Richard's armour, probably a symbolic gesture intended to spur faithful men into military action.[50]

The regents responded accordingly. By this stage it must have been clear that the danger of invasion from Flanders had passed; a few foreign ships had attempted to make a landing but their crews had been captured by the coastal levies. John's forces, meanwhile, had been confined to two main castles – Windsor in the south and Tickhill in the north – and towards the end of March both were placed under siege. Royal financial records reveal that over 1,000 men were deployed at Windsor, while three shiploads of stone were sent up the Thames to provide ammunition for the siege engines. Even once these assaults were under way, however, there were still signs of hesitancy. One chronicler accused Walter of Coutances of laxity in prosecuting the siege of Windsor because he had relatives among the defenders. In the north some magnates refused to join in the attack on Tickhill, asserting that 'they were liegemen of Count John', a refusal that led the archbishop of York to brand them 'traitors to the king and the kingdom'. Yet while the king himself remained out of his kingdom, the conflict of loyalties continued.[51]

What eventually ended both sieges was the arrival in England on 20 April of another of Richard's crusading companions, Hubert Walter. Hubert had been sent from the king's side to begin his career as archbishop of Canterbury – his appointment being in part a reward for the strenuous efforts he had already made in trying to procure Richard's release. He also came to assist the regency government in the Herculean task of raising the king's ransom, the working figure for which was 100,000 marks. Such a colossal sum could not be accumulated while money was pouring from the treasury to pay for the assault against John's castles, nor could it be collected in full unless John would allow royal agents to enter his own lands. Despite the fact that both Windsor and Tickhill were reportedly on the verge of surrender, a truce was agreed until the autumn. John gave up Windsor and Wallingford to his mother, but was allowed to retain Tickhill and Nottingham.[52]

All John's hopes must have now been pinned on Philip Augustus, whose attack on Normandy had enjoyed much greater success. Although deterred from besieging Rouen by the bravado of its citizens, he had succeeded in taking several major strongholds along the Norman border. Having achieved all he could for the time being by military means, he now engaged in a diplomatic struggle with Richard's regents; as they laboured to raise money for the king's ransom, so he sought to ensure that his rival would be detained indefinitely. A meeting between the French king and the emperor was scheduled for 25 June, though in the event Richard himself managed to persuade Henry not to attend by agreeing to increase the ransom by a further 50,000 marks. (One of the remarkable aspects of Richard's captivity was the skill with which he was able to charm and win over his captors.) When Philip heard tell of this latest twist in early July, he sent a despairing message to his ally in England, saying, 'Look to yourself, the Devil is loosed!' John, fearing his brother's return was imminent, fled across the Channel and sought refuge at Philip's court.[53]

In fact Richard's release still waited on the raising of his ransom, a process that would take many months. The government in England strained every sinew, demanding a quarter of the wealth of the clergy and the laity in tax, stripping the altar plate from churches and confiscating the entire wool crop of the Cistercian monks. A separate exchequer was set up to process the money as it poured in, and the sacks of silver were stored in St Paul's Cathedral. In the meantime Philip Augustus tried to resurrect his scheme to invade England. Hoping to secure more powerful naval support, he allied with King Cnut VI of Denmark by marrying his daughter, Ingeborg. Alas for Philip (and even more so for Ingeborg), their wedding night in August was such a disaster that he tried, without success, to hand her back to the Danish ambassadors the very next morning. All the episode gained him was years of domestic grief and condemnation from the Church for refusing to recognize his new queen.[54]

Quite what Philip's relationship with John was like by this point is more difficult to ascertain, but theirs too was a marriage of convenience rather than any genuine affection. John, for his part, seems to have tried to conceal the fact that he had given permission for Richard's ransom to be collected on his English estates. Philip, according to the more dubious *History of William Marshal*, was 'completely dismissive' of his Angevin house guest and 'thought him a fool'. Certainly Richard had hopes of parting the pair, for at some stage in the autumn he sent an offer to his brother, promising to restore all his possessions if he would renew his allegiance. John accepted, and travelled to Normandy, but at that point the plan backfired. So low had John's reputation sunk that the royal agents keeping his castles refused to hand them over, even when they were shown Richard's written orders to do so. John returned enraged to Philip's court.[55]

By 20 December 1193 so much treasure had been shipped to Germany that Henry VI declared himself satisfied, and announced that Richard would be released on 17 January 1194. Then, shortly after Christmas, envoys arrived from John and Philip with a range of last-minute counter-offers, including £1,000 a month to keep Richard captive or £100,000 to hand him over. ('See how much they loved him!' said Roger of Howden acidly.) John had by now become utterly desperate: it was also around this point that he made a fresh treaty with Philip, agreeing to surrender huge portions of the Angevin Empire if the French king would recognize him as its ruler and help him obtain it. The emperor was sufficiently tempted by these new proposals to postpone Richard's release date and show him the letters from Philip and John, which reportedly caused the king to despair of ever being liberated. But when Henry convened the bishops and princes of the empire to discuss these new bids, they reproved him for trying to back out of his existing agreement. On 4 February 1194, Richard was freed.[56]

The news spelt the end for John. Back in England Hubert Walter, lately invested as archbishop of Canterbury and appointed as the new justiciar, declared him excommunicate. The regency government, having left John's garrisons unmolested during the winter despite the expiry of the earlier truce, now abandoned their pragmatic caution and renewed their attack on his castles.[57] Most had already surrendered by the time Richard landed in England on 13 March (news of his arrival reportedly caused one of John's supporters, the keeper of St Michael's Mount, to die of fright). Only at Nottingham did the defenders hold out until the king himself appeared outside the walls, eventually capitulating on 28 March. Three days later in a council held in the castle's great hall, Richard demanded judgement 'against Count John his brother, who, contrary to the fealty he had sworn him, had occupied his castles, laid waste his lands on both sides of the sea, and made a treaty against him with his enemy, the king of France'. John was given forty days to present himself, on pain of forfeiting any future claim to the kingdom.[58]

Richard then went south: on 17 April he was ceremoniously re-crowned in Winchester Cathedral, and on 12 May he crossed the Channel to Normandy. In the weeks since his liberation, John and Philip Augustus had once again invaded the duchy and captured yet more castles; when Richard arrived they were laying siege to Verneuil. According to *The History of William Marshal*, as the king was advancing to confront them, he stopped for the night in Lisieux, where he lodged in the house of his friend, the local archdeacon. Noting that his host was ill at ease, he quickly deduced what the problem was, saying, 'You've seen my brother John,' then adding, 'Let him come forward, and have no fear of me.' A short time later a trembling John appeared and fell at his brother's feet. It had been over four years since they had last seen one another face to face – John was now twenty-seven years old, Richard thirty-six – but the nature of their relationship remained unaltered. Raising his younger brother up by the hand, the king gave him a magnanimous kiss of peace. 'Have no fear, John, you are a child, and were left with bad guardians ... Go and have something to eat,' Richard added, sending his brother away to dine on a freshly caught salmon.[59]

5

Stemming the Tide

1205–1206

John sailed into Studland Bay in Dorset on 16 June 1205, presumably still furious about the collapse of the great expedition that he had hoped would recover his lost continental territories. Perhaps to occupy himself as much as for any other reason, he headed west to Dartmouth, where the subsidiary force under the command of his bastard son Geoffrey was still preparing to leave for Poitou. Geoffrey probably put to sea on 22 June, for at that point the king headed inland to spend a fortnight at his favourite castles and hunting lodges in Dorset and Wiltshire. Whatever solace he found during this time must have been diminished by the news that on 23 June his great ancestral castle at Chinon had finally surrendered to the forces of Philip Augustus, meaning that his very last toehold of territory in Anjou had been lost.[1]

A few days later, however, John received a message that apparently brightened his mood. The archbishop of Canterbury, Hubert Walter – the man who, along with William Marshal, had done the most to frustrate his planned expedition – was dead. The cause of his death, according to Ralph of Coggeshall, was a growth near his groin that he had been too embarrassed to have treated. The king, according to Roger of Wendover, was delighted. 'By God's feet!' he cried. 'Now for the first time I am king and lord of England!' These are actually the words of the chronicler

Matthew Paris, writing twenty years later, who liked them so much he has John say them again on the death of another royal minister in 1213. Yet there can be little doubt that both Paris and Wendover were right to imagine that the king was genuinely pleased. Hubert had been Richard's choice as archbishop and chief justiciar. He had excommunicated John in 1194 and helped to crush his rebellion. John may have appointed him as chancellor at the start of his reign, but this was probably to reassure those who doubted the new king's competence rather than his own personal preference. As far as John was concerned, the arch-bishop's recent actions must have proved he was an impediment to progress. Now he was gone, the king stood a much better chance of getting his own way.[2]

Hubert had died on 13 July at his manor of Teynham in Kent, at which point John was in Buckinghamshire. But by 15 July the king had arrived in Canterbury, his haste a measure of his anxiety to ensure that the right man was elected as Hubert's replacement. In theory, and especially since Henry II's clash with Thomas Becket, cathedral clergy were free to choose their own bishops, but in reality bishops were too politically important for their appointment to be left to local democracy. Normally kings would find a way of making their wishes known in order to ensure that their preferred candidate was selected. 'We order you to hold a free election,' wrote Henry II to the monks of Winchester Cathedral in 1172, 'but we nevertheless forbid you to elect anyone except Richard, our clerk.' Six years into his reign, by similar if perhaps more subtle means, John had generally been successful in getting the bishops he wanted.[3]

The complicating factor at Canterbury was that it was an archbishopric: whoever was appointed to that particular role had authority not just over his own diocese but over almost all the other bishops in England. (The exceptions were the bishops of Carlisle and Durham, who answered to the archbishop of York.) These other bishops, not unreasonably, felt that they should have some say in choosing their superior, but the monks of Canterbury thought otherwise, and insisted that the right to choose a new archbishop belonged to them alone. Of course, such arguments would only arise on occasions when the bishops and the monks were unable to agree on a mutually acceptable candidate, but that was evidently the case in 1205: by the time John arrived in Canterbury, the two sides were already deadlocked. The only way forward was to put the long-standing dispute about who had the superior right to elect to the judgement of the pope. The king therefore asked the prior and monks to postpone the election until the end of November, by which time they could hope to have received a papal verdict. According to one of their number, the chronicler Gervase of Canterbury, he spoke kindly to the monks, 'and gave them some hope that they could have someone from their own church'.[4]

If this was indeed the case, it is an example of John being completely disingenuous, for he already had in mind a non-monastic candidate. John de Gray was a clerk who had served the king loyally since before his accession. He had acted as the keeper of the king's seal from 1198, and had been rewarded two years later by being appointed as bishop of Norwich. He was attached to his royal master, said Roger of Wendover, 'by a great intimacy, and was the only one among the prelates of England who knew his private affairs'. John now intended to advance him to the top position in the English church, and to this end he secretly sent messengers of his own to Rome, hoping to persuade the pope to confirm his candidate, and so present the monks of Canterbury with a fait accompli.[5]

But, as Gervase of Canterbury explains, the monks got wind of the king's underhand scheme and responded with a little subterfuge of their own. With equal secrecy they elected their sub-prior, Reginald, and sent him to Rome with five companions. All of them had taken an oath not to reveal the nature of their business unless the pope was on the point of yielding to John's request, but in the event they acted more precipitately. As soon as they reached the Curia (or as soon as they were across the Channel, if we believe Roger of Wendover), Reginald was telling people that he had been elected as the new archbishop.

The king's agents in Rome and the bishops' representatives protested, and sent news of this unexpected development back to England.[6]

Travel between England and Rome took at least a month in the Middle Ages, and it was not until late November that the news reached John. He immediately returned to Canterbury at the start of December and demanded to know whether it was true that the monks had held an election in spite of their earlier promise not to do so. Evidently he spoke less kindly on this occasion than before: later papal letters suggest that the monks feared 'the loss of their property and danger to their persons'. In the face of the king's wrath they assured him that no election had taken place, and to placate him still further they dropped their appeal to Rome. John then rode to London to obtain a similar renunciation from the bishops, before returning to Canterbury a week later in the company of John de Gray, whom the monks obligingly elected as their new archbishop, and led ceremoniously into the cathedral to be seated on his archiepiscopal throne. Both the king and the bishops then sent letters to the pope, explaining that John de Gray had been elected 'for the honour and profit of the church of Canterbury, and the king, and the whole kingdom of England'.[7]

While his agents in Rome had been labouring to resolve his local difficulties in Canterbury, John's thoughts had rarely strayed from the greater, overriding problem of how to recover his lost lands in France. His immediate concern in 1205 was not with the northern territories of Normandy and Anjou, where everything had now been lost to the king of France, but the southern duchy of Aquitaine. In Poitou (the northern part of Aquitaine) the situation was extremely bad. The nobility there had deserted to Philip in August the previous year, and only the fortified seaport of La Rochelle continued to hold out. Meanwhile Gascony (the southern part of the duchy) had been all but taken over by Alfonso VIII, king of Castile, the greatest of the several kingdoms that made up medieval Spain. Back in 1177 Alfonso had married

John's sister, Eleanor, and it had been agreed that, after the death of her namesake mother, she would have Gascony as her dower. That at any rate was what the Castilian king claimed in the autumn of 1204, and set out to make good his claim by leading an army across the Pyrenees and occupying almost the whole region. Only a handful of towns – most notably Bordeaux – held out against this new onslaught; John wrote to thank the citizens for their good service at the end of April 1205. Throughout the rest of the year he remained in constant communication with his few remaining overseas subjects. In June, soon after the dispatch of his bastard son Geoffrey, he had sent another force of knights to Poitou under the captaincy of his half-brother William, earl of Salisbury (another of Henry II's bastards, to whom John seems to have been close), and in early October some Poitevin knights had come to visit him in England. According to Ralph of Coggeshall the king gave 28,000 marks to the brother of the archbishop of Bordeaux with which to raise a 30,000-man army. These figures look suspiciously high, but at the start of the new year 1206 arrangements were being made to ship large amounts of money to Poitou – royal letters mention sums totalling 2,500 marks.[8]

Money remained a major worry. Clearly an enormous amount had been wasted on the expedition of 1205 that had never sailed. (Royal records suggest a figure of around £2,200, but the true total was almost certainly a great deal higher.) To put together a similar force would require a sum of the same magnitude to be raised all over again. Added to this was the continuing problem of inflation. The partial re-coinage that John had carried out to combat rising prices during the winter of 1204–5 had been only partially successful: the rise in prices had been slowed down, but prices remained stubbornly high. Henry II and Richard had paid their mercenary knights a wage of eightpence a day, but John was having to offer three times as much (two shillings a day) to secure the same service. Such a steep hike meant that to mount an effective campaign more money than ever would have to be found, but doing so would be difficult. Immediately after the collapse of the 1205 expedition John had levied yet another payment in lieu of military service, or scutage, and this would eventually bring in a useful £4,000. But scutage had already proved politically contentious, particularly in the north of England, where opposition to the previous levy had led to its collection being abandoned earlier in the year. Moreover, the sums raised by scutage, while respectable, were not in themselves sufficient to fund a major campaign. Other sources of money would have to be exploited.[9]

In every county (or shire) in England, the king had a variety of agents who raised money on his behalf, the most important of whom was the sheriff (or shire reeve). Sheriffs raised money in a number of different ways: they collected rents from the king's own lands and the profits of justice from the county court, and they levied a tax known as 'sheriff's aid'. But however much a sheriff raised, he paid the king a lump sum, fixed by long tradition. Such fixed sums were known as 'farms' (from the Latin *firma*, 'fixed'), and the men who collected them were farmers. Thus the sheriff was a farmer responsible for collecting the county farm.

Traditionally, the biggest part of the county farm had come from the rents received from the king's own lands (the royal demesne). The problem by John's day was that the king's lands were nothing like as extensive as they had once been. Back in the time of Henry I, the royal demesne had been vast, but during the civil war between Stephen and Matilda it had been greatly depleted, as both sides gave away land to retain their supporters, while other magnates simply helped themselves to royal property. Henry II had arrested this trend and by the end of his reign had succeeded in clawing some land back, but Richard had quickly undone his father's work, selling or granting away lands to secure support for his crusade. ('I would sell London, if only I could find a buyer,' he is alleged to have quipped.) The drop in revenue was dramatic: at Henry's death in 1189 the county farms had been worth sixty per cent of their original value; by the time Richard died in 1199, so great were his alienations, the figure had fallen to just thirty-nine per cent.

On his return to England in 1194 Richard (or perhaps his new chief minister, Hubert Walter) had sought to increase the Crown's revenue by demanding that some sheriffs pay an additional sum, above the county farm, known as an 'increment'. This was tried in the case of nine counties, and although it succeeded in raising more cash, it proved highly unpopular. With less money coming in from Crown lands, the sheriffs had to find the extra money from other sources, increasing the amount they took in local taxes or judicial fines. John had maintained these increments, but he increasingly found that sheriffs were unable, or unwilling, to pay them in full.[10]

And so, in the autumn of 1204, John (or, again, perhaps Hubert Walter) had tried a new experiment. In the majority of counties, the king demanded not only the traditional farm, but all the money that the sheriff had raised above and beyond it.[11] At a time of rapidly rising prices, this was a sensible expedient. Many private landlords had by this date abandoned the practice of leasing out their estates for a fixed sum, and had instead begun to manage their lands directly, thereby netting all the surpluses that a farmer would have pocketed. At the same time, pocketing the profits of a county was what made the office of sheriff attractive. In introducing a system that made the sheriff simply a custodian of the Crown's lands, the government clearly found it difficult (or felt it risky) to retain the services of powerful and well-connected men, many of whom were replaced in their posts at this moment with local men who possessed less political clout. Nevertheless, in financial terms, John's experiment was a success. For the first six years of his reign the county farms had brought in an average of £4,000 a year, but in 1205 that total rose to over £5,000, and thereafter it was maintained at an average of £5,725 a year.

Important as this increase was, the revenue raised by the sheriffs amounted to only around fifteen to twenty per cent of all royal income in any given year. One simple way in which the king could raise additional sums of money was to sell offices. The office of sheriff, for example, was frequently sold to the highest

bidder. Sometimes a man close to the king would buy a sheriffdom with the intention of recouping his investment, and more
besides, from the shire in question. In 1201, for example, William
de Stuteville (one of the northern barons who had refused to
besiege Tickhill in 1193, saying he was John's liegeman) had
bought the sheriffdom of Yorkshire for £1,113. In other cases,
men of a particular shire might collectively offer the king a large
sum of money to have their own choice of sheriff, precisely to
escape the harsher financial regime that a voracious outsider
would invariably try to impose. Thus in 1205 Thomas de Moulton
became the new sheriff of Lincoln with the backing of the local
gentry in return for a payment to the king of 500 marks and
five palfreys.[12]

It was not just sheriffdoms that were sold. 'Everything was put
up for sale', commented Roger of Howden of the great auction
at the start of Richard's reign. 'Offices, lordships, earldoms, sheriffdoms, castles, towns, lands, the lot.' John may not have been
quite so eager to sell, especially after 1204,[13] but he was always
willing to strike a deal if the price was right. When Hubert Walter
died in 1205 the king needed to find not only a new archbishop
but also a new chancellor. In October that year the latter post
was filled by Walter de Gray, nephew of the bishop of Norwich,
a young man whose qualifications for the role were almost non-
existent, but who was sufficiently confident of the money he
would be able to make that he agreed to pay the king 5,000
marks for the privilege.

If offices could be sold, so too could justice. This is not quite
as negative as it sounds. Henry II had greatly extended the reach
of royal justice, sending his judges on regular tours around the
country to hear cases, and introducing standard civil pleas that
could be initiated by the purchase of an inexpensive writ. These
moves were extremely popular, though they did nothing for the
king's coffers, because the small sums charged went to the chancellor (which was one of the reasons the post was so lucrative).[14]

But not all justice was routine, nor could all of it be delegated.
Men who held their lands directly from the king (tenants-in-

chief, which generally meant the barons) had no choice but to have their cases heard in the king's own court, while others might choose to bring their case before the king in the hope of obtaining swift and decisive judgement. Wherever he was, the king would always have some judges with him, and would himself act as supreme judge when the necessity arose. There is plentiful evidence to indicate that John, like his father, knew the law well, consulted his judges on matters of controversy, and deferred to them on points of detail.

At this level, however, justice was inextricably mixed with politics. The king might refuse to hear the suit of an individual he disliked, for example, or he might delay a case for years on end rather than give judgement against a man whose support he needed. Consequently great men sought to grease the wheels of the system by offering large sums of money, often running into four figures. In 1200 William de Stuteville had offered John 3,000 marks to receive his 'right' in an inheritance dispute; his opponent, William of Mowbray, made a counter-offer of 2,000 marks 'to be treated justly according to the custom of England'. The beauty of this arrangement from the king's point of view was that he did not even have to demand such colossal sums – men would offer them freely, trying to outbid each other in the hope of obtaining a favourable verdict.[15]

Lastly, the king could raise large amounts of money on a regular basis in his capacity as a lord. Since the Norman Conquest, the kings of England had enjoyed an exceptional degree of control over the lives of their greatest subjects. If a tenant-in-chief died, for example, and his heir or heirs were underage, the king became their guardian, and they his wards; the king retained their estates until they came of age, and had the right to arrange their marriages as he saw fit. Similarly, if a tenant-in-chief died leaving a widow, the king had the right to find her a new husband. To modern ears these sound like outrageous infringements of individual freedom but, as in the case of justice, the lives of the baronage were bound up in politics. The king's greatest subjects held vast estates, and also castles – the raw instruments of political power.

The king could not afford to see these pass into the hands of his enemies through the unpredictable accidents of birth, death and marriage.[16]

These 'feudal' powers of the king had always offered an opportunity for profit. To enter into his inheritance, an heir had to pay a sum known as a 'relief'; in the case of underage heirs, the king retained not only their estates but also all the profits arising from them for the duration of the wardship. And there had always been a flourishing market at court for the marriages of both wards and widows. The king could reward his friends with the hand of a wealthy heiress or dowager, or simply sell the right to marry either to the highest bidder.[17]

Under the Angevins, however, the financial exploitation of these rights had increased dramatically. Henry II may have kept his demands moderate: on the nine occasions when he could have charged a relief for an earldom, for instance, he chose to do so only once. His sons, by contrast, showed no such moderation. At a time when the baronage felt that £100 was a reasonable figure, Richard had demanded reliefs of 500 marks and 1,000 marks. One northern baron, Eustace de Vescy, was charged 1,300 marks to have his inheritance, even though the Crown had enjoyed its profits during an eight-year wardship. John had set reliefs at a similar eye-watering level, typically charging 600 marks.[18] In the same way, proffers for the right to marry wards and widows had begun to rocket, so that they resembled the four-figure sums that were being offered for 'justice'. Widows could avoid remarriage if they wished, provided that they could keep up with the bidding. Thus in 1205 the estates of Alice Belet were seized when she refused to wed a man who had offered the king fifty marks and two palfreys for her hand; she regained possession when her father offered to pay 100 marks for her right to remain single. Amabilia, widow of the northern baron Hugh Bardolf, similarly beat off a £1,000 bid for her marriage by agreeing to pay the king 2,000 marks.[19]

By such expedients – fiscal, judicial and feudal – John and his immediate predecessors had pushed up their regular income, even though the amount of land they possessed had plummeted since the days of their Norman ancestors. Astute contemporaries were aware of the shift. 'One may marvel that Henry II and his sons, despite their many wars, nevertheless abounded in wealth', wrote Gerald of Wales. 'The reason is that they took care to augment their revenue from rents with casual income, and relied more on subsidiary than basic sources of profit.' The figures show that, since the loss of Normandy in 1204, John had been very successful augmenting his wealth in this way. In the opening years of his reign his income had averaged about £23,000 a year, but in 1205 and 1206 that average had risen to about £30,000 – a figure more than sufficient to fund a campaign to Poitou of the kind the king had in mind.[20]

The question that remained was whether John could muster the necessary political support, or whether he would end up repeating the humiliating scenes of the previous summer, when the baronage had refused to follow him. At the highest level, his position looked promising. Hubert Walter, the chief obstacle in 1205, lay dead and buried in Canterbury Cathedral. The new archbishop-elect, John de Gray, was the king's close confidant, and the new chancellor was Gray's nephew, Walter. As for John's other main opponent from the previous year, William Marshal, he was nothing like as removed from the king's inner circle as his biographer would have us believe. When John celebrated Christmas 1205 in Oxford, for example, the Marshal was there celebrating with him, as was the king's half-brother William, earl of Salisbury, along with Ranulf, earl of Chester, and the earls of Essex and Surrey. Clearly this was a king who could still command the support of his greatest men.[21]

The question was whether he could also command the support of the wider baronage. Soon after Christmas, in January 1206, John set out once again for the north of England. The main reason for this journey was a meeting with the king of Scots, about which we know nothing, but presumably arranged to ensure cordial relations would be maintained in the event that John did indeed leave the country. But while he was in the north John travelled widely, visiting his castles at Richmond, Carlisle, Lancaster and Chester, and during this tour he must have come face to face with many of his northern barons. The kind of pressure he could bring to bear on these men is well illustrated by the visit he paid in mid-February to his newly acquired castle at Knaresborough in North Yorkshire. For forty years down to 1203, Knaresborough had been in the possession of the aforementioned William de Stuteville, who had obtained it after its previous keeper had rebelled against Henry II in 1173. In 1203, however, William had died, and was soon followed to the grave by his underage son and heir – at which point John had pounced. In August 1205 he allowed the Stuteville inheritance to pass to William's brother, Nicholas, but in return he demanded a gargantuan relief of 10,000 marks. The point on this occasion was not to obtain payment, but the surrender of Knaresborough Castle, which the king retained as security for Nicholas' massive debt.[22] Knaresborough was one of the most strategically important fortresses in northern England; John immediately committed it to one of his most trusted military captains, Brian de Lisle, and began to invest large sums improving its defences. Part of his reason for visiting in February 1206 was presumably to see how this work was progressing. Precisely what Nicholas de Stuteville thought of this arrangement is hard to say, but in the short term it kept him obedient. When John mustered his forces for a new expedition to Poitou in the spring of 1206, Nicholas was one of the many northern barons who dutifully turned out.[23]

Advance preparations for the new campaign had been under way for some time. In London shipwrights had worked throughout the winter to build the king eight new transport ships, and in the early spring siege equipment was being manufactured in the forests of Sussex. The temporary wooden towers and galleries known as 'brattices' were already being shipped to the Channel Islands, which had been briefly lost to the French in 1204 but recovered by English forces the following year, and which obviously formed an important staging post on the sea route to Aquitaine.

In the last days of April, at which point John was in London, a flurry of writs showed that preparations were entering their final phase. On 29 April royal officials in Southampton were ordered to seize all the ships in neighbouring ports capable of carrying eight or more horses for a muster at Portsmouth on 20 May. When the king himself arrived on the Hampshire coast a few days in advance of this deadline, however, it was clear that not enough vessels had been found: on 19 May officials on the Channel Islands were ordered to send agents out into the southern shipping lanes 'who knew how to talk wisely and warmly to the steersmen and sailors, to move and induce them to come quickly into our service, and to assure them of our peace and goodwill and safe conduct'. By the end of the month more than 200 ships and some 2,100 sailors were assembled at Portsmouth, ready to transport the tonnes of supplies and thousands of soldiers that had been building up during the previous fortnight. On 28 May John crossed the Solent to the Isle of Wight, and at the start of June he set sail for Aquitaine.[24]

A week or so later, on 8 June, the king and his fleet put in to the great harbour of La Rochelle, to the relief of the locals who had held out so long and so loyally for this moment. Thanks to their efforts, bolstered by the troops and the money that the king had dispatched throughout the previous year, the military situation was not quite as desperate as it had been twelve months earlier. Towards the end of 1205 the town of Niort, forty miles inland to the east, had been recovered, and thereby become the new front line in the struggle against the supporters of Philip Augustus. John's first move was to advance in this direction, perhaps scattering any besieging forces, for he marched beyond Niort and a further fifteen miles towards Poitiers.[25]

Having relieved his subjects in Poitou, he turned his army south, consolidating his hold on the region around the town of Saintes before advancing further south into Gascony. Here too his local supporters had done much of the work ahead of his arrival. King Alfonso of Castile, having failed to take Bordeaux by siege, had by this stage withdrawn from Gascony altogether, reportedly complaining about the poverty of the region and the fickleness of its inhabitants; by the summer of 1206 the only remaining Spanish presence in the region was the garrison ensconced on the north bank of the Gironde at Bourg-sur-Mer, and these troops soon surrendered, apparently to local forces.[26]

John's army did, however, win one notable victory. Although Alfonso himself had returned home, he had enjoyed considerable support from among the Gascon nobility, and these men had shut themselves up in Montauban, a fortified town on the duchy's eastern border. Montauban was a fortress famous in song and legend; Charlemagne, it was said, had failed to take it despite a siege that had lasted seven years. Contemporaries were impressed, therefore, when John's army succeeded in taking it in a matter of days. After a fortnight of bombardment by siege engines, explains Roger of Wendover, the castle fell to a direct assault, with English troops scaling the walls and fighting hand to hand until their enemies surrendered. John sent exultant letters back to England, naming the many nobles who had been taken prisoner and describing the prodigious spoils that had been seized.[27]

With resistance in Gascony at an end, the king retraced his steps northwards towards Niort, arriving there on or around 21 August. One week later, perhaps emboldened by his success in the south, he set out to try to win back some of the territory that had been lost to Philip Augustus. From Niort he marched his forces eighty miles east across Poitou to the border with Berry, and then almost double that distance west until he reached the border with Brittany. These manoeuvres persuaded the most powerful nobleman in the region, the viscount of Thouars, to renew his allegiance to John, a signal victory which spurred the king to try his luck further. In early September he advanced with his new ally into Anjou, and successfully forded the River Loire – a feat 'such as was never heard of in our time', according to a local chronicler. For a whole week he held court in Angers, home of his Angevin forefathers, before marching even further north in mid–September as far as the border with Maine.[28]

By this point, however, Philip Augustus had been stirred into action. No doubt alarmed by John's rapid success, the French king raised an army and marched towards Poitou. John, no doubt alarmed in turn, decided it was time to sound the retreat; over the course of the next three weeks he cautiously made his way back south, reaching Niort by 12 October. Caution, indeed, seems to have been the watchword on both sides. Philip advanced his army to the Poitevin border but no further; for the time being he had his hands full in Normandy and was content to allow John his recent gains. John, for his part, was not yet ready for a direct confrontation with his principal opponent. The aim of his present expedition had been to preserve his position in Aquitaine, and that objective had been achieved. Accordingly, on 26 October, a two-year truce was sealed. Both kings agreed to maintain the territorial and political status quo, and in the meantime to permit travellers and merchants to move freely between their dominions.[29]

With the truce in place, John returned to La Rochelle in early November, then moved to the adjacent Ile de Ré, from where he set sail in the middle of the month. After several weeks carefully negotiating the treacherous coast of Brittany, his fleet finally put into Portsmouth on 12 December. 'When he arrived home,' says *The History of William Marshal*, 'he was given a welcome by many who loved him and cherished him and paid him high honour as they greeted him.' The following day the sheriff of Hampshire was instructed to find 1,500 hens, 5,000 eggs, 20 oxen, 100 pigs and 100 sheep, the makings of what must have been the merriest Christmas feast at John's court for several years.[30]

6

Our Happy Success

1194–1202

In trying to usurp his brother's throne, John had done terrible damage to his reputation. His failure in Ireland might have been put down to youthful inexperience; his desertion of his dying father explained as unfortunate timing. That men were prepared to overlook these earlier mistakes is suggested by their readiness to rally behind him in 1191 when he challenged the rule of the justiciar William Longchamp. For a moment he had been a popular hero, saving the realm from tyrannical oppression, in return for which he had been recognized as Richard's rightful heir. But John had gone on to overplay his hand and lost spectacularly. No one could excuse the behaviour of a man who had attempted to seize the kingdom of an imprisoned crusader. By rebelling against Richard, said William of Newburgh, John had simply succeeded in 'heaping up endless curses on his own perfidious head'. He was a 'mad-headed youth' who had broken 'the laws of nature', and become 'nature's enemy'.[1]

The damage to his position was equally catastrophic. Within days of Richard's release from captivity the regency government had stripped John of all his lands and titles in both England and Normandy; Richard, although he subsequently accepted his brother's submission, refused to reverse this verdict. Apart from his title 'lord of Ireland', which appears to have been a empty designation by this point, John had lost everything. His household was deliberately broken up, and those of his followers who had supported his rebellion found themselves similarly deprived of their lands and property.[2]

Had John also lost his position as heir apparent? In the period 1191–2 the political community in England had repeatedly sworn to recognize him as Richard's successor. In March 1194, after his brother's return, John had been warned he would lose all claim to the kingdom if he did not submit within forty days – a deadline he had failed to meet. Nothing official was subsequently said to clarify the issue. Richard's last known statement on the matter, back in 1190, was that his nephew, Arthur of Brittany, should succeed him. Whether or not that was still his wish is unknown. Richard, now freed from captivity and able to resume conjugal relations with his queen, probably hoped that in due course he would be succeeded by a son of his own. Whatever the king's intentions were, John's position with regard to the throne must have seemed very weak in 1194, his future – beyond perhaps a role in Ireland – in grave doubt.[3]

The only hope of recovery lay in faithful service. Richard's overriding concern from the spring of 1194 was the recovery of the lands that had been lost during his captivity to Philip Augustus. John, of course, had been the French king's willing co-conspirator in seizing these lands, and he was able to score an immediate success by returning to Evreux – a town given to him by Philip – and slaughtering the garrison before they realized he had switched sides. Whether this did anything to improve his standing with Richard is unclear, but it compounded his reputation for treachery in France, and provoked an angry response from Philip, who sacked the town in revenge. Late in the summer, while Richard was winning back territory in Touraine and Aquitaine, John was left in Normandy to besiege the French forces occupying Vaudreuil. Philip, beaten by Richard in the south, rushed north to vent his fury on John for a second time, falling on his camp at dawn and forcing him to flee, with the loss of most of his infantry and siege equipment.[4]

Despite its apparently limited results, John's military service impressed contemporaries – William of Newburgh commends him for fighting against Philip 'faithfully and valiantly' – and eventually caused Richard to soften his stance. In 1195, according to Roger of Howden, the king 'forgave his brother John all the wrath and displeasure he felt towards him', and restored some of his lands and titles: the county of Mortain, the earldom of Gloucester and the honour of Eye in Suffolk were all handed back, and John was also promised an annual payment of £2,000. He did not, however, regain custody of any of his castles. Richard's trust in his younger brother clearly still had its limits.[5]

With regard to the succession, too, John's position improved, largely due to Richard's botched attempt to tighten his grip on Brittany. The Angevins regarded Brittany as a dependency, but the duchy had been left to go its own way since the death of Henry II; in 1196 Richard tried to reassert this traditional mastery by obtaining custody of its young duke, Arthur. His plan miscarried, however, when Arthur's mother, Constance, was kidnapped en route to the king's court by her estranged second husband. The nobles of Brittany, suspecting that this was a plot on Richard's part, refused to hand Arthur over, and appealed for help to Philip Augustus; Richard responded by invading Brittany and crushing all resistance, but failed to apprehend his nephew, who was successfully conveyed to the French king. Clearly there was no way Arthur could be groomed as Richard's heir if he was Philip's ally. Moreover, by 1196, it was looking increasingly unlikely that Richard was going to father a son. Two chroniclers accused him of being unfaithful to his queen and neglecting to sleep with her. If only by default, John was once again coming to be regarded as first in line. There was no public avowal of his position, as there had been during Richard's absence, but in private the king seems to have accepted the fact. Documents drawn up in the autumn of 1197 – one concerning the construction of Château Gaillard – show John guaranteeing to uphold his brother's agreements.[6]

And yet, despite his apparent rehabilitation, John's reputation was such that suspicion could easily be rekindled. Although he appears to have served Richard loyally during 1198, fighting

against Philip Augustus when war re-erupted that autumn, relations between the two brothers collapsed early in 1199, when
the French king wrote to Richard to inform him that John had
once again defected. Whether there was any truth in this is
impossible to determine. By this point Arthur had repudiated
Philip and returned to Brittany, and the Bretons had returned
to Richard's allegiance. John may well have been alarmed by
these developments and sought to counter their implications by
plotting with Philip. Roger of Howden dismissed the accusations
as a piece of malicious invention on the French king's part, but
admits that Richard believed what he was told and again deprived
John of all his lands in both England and Normandy. Two other
chroniclers report that John remained dispossessed and out of
favour in the spring of 1199, right up to the moment when
Richard was hit by a crossbow bolt.[7]

It happened in Aquitaine, at an obscure little castle called Châlus-
Chabrol, about twenty miles south-east of Limoges. Rumour said
Richard had gone there to claim some treasure that a peasant
had ploughed up in a field, but the real reason was a rebellion
by two of his leading vassals in the region, the viscount of Limoges
and his half-brother, the count of Angoulême. By 1199 Richard
was clearly winning the war against Philip Augustus; he had won
back almost all the lost ground in Normandy, and held more
territory along the Loire than at the start of his reign. But Philip
had struck back by allying with these two southern nobles and
encouraging them to revolt. The castle at Châlus belonged to the
viscount of Limoges and Richard held it in little regard. He was
besieging it when a lone crossbowman, reduced to using a frying
pan as a shield, shot him in the shoulder. A surgeon managed to
remove the bolt, but butchered the king's flesh so badly that the
wound turned gangrenous. Eleven days later he was dead.[8]

The sudden death of the great warrior forced the question of
who would succeed him. The debates men must have been
having in private for years suddenly required urgent resolution.
Who had the greater right: John or Arthur? *The History of William*

Marshal relates a splendid scene, clearly much improved with hindsight, in which the Marshal himself learns of Richard's death four days after the event. He was staying in the castle at Rouen, and about to go to bed, when the news arrived, prompting him to pull his boots back on and seek out the archbishop of Canterbury, Hubert Walter, who was lodged in the nearby priory. After exchanging words of grief, their conversation turned quickly to the succession. Hubert opined that Arthur had the greater right, while the Marshal argued that John was nearest in line. But the reality was that the legal merits of the two claims, being debatable, hardly mattered: fundamentally the question came down to personalities and politics. 'Arthur has treacherous advisers about him, and he is haughty and overbearing,' says the Marshal. 'If we call him to our side he will seek to do us harm and damage, for he does not like those in our realm.' This was the crux of the matter: whether those who lived under Plantagenet rule wanted to see it endure in its existing form, or some compromised, truncated version. The Marshal speaks as a representative of the Anglo-Norman baronage ('our side') who wished to preserve the empire as it was, and with it their own cross-Channel holdings. But there were others – traitors in William Marshal's view – who would have been more than happy to see that empire broken up: not only the nobles of Brittany, who had long resented Plantagenet overlordship, but also nobles in other regions who had come to resent the rule of Henry II and Richard. There was also, of course, Philip Augustus, who had already indicated his readiness to collaborate with Arthur and to help the Bretons achieve their aim of throwing off the Plantagenet yoke. In addition to all this, there was the simple factor of age: even if Arthur had possessed the willingness to defend Plantagenet power and resist Philip, he was only twelve years old at the time of Richard's death – no match for the experienced and wily French king. In these circumstances, for those who wished to keep things as they were, the only possible candidate was John. He may have made a poor showing of himself in the past, but he was a grown man, and was also 'one of us', who would be committed to maintaining the whole of his inheritance. In *The History of William Marshal* Hubert Walter eventually defers to the Marshal's judgement on the matter, but prophesies that John will be a disaster. 'This much I can tell you,' he says to the earl, 'you will never come to regret anything you did as much as what you're doing now.'[9]

With opinion divided across the Plantagenet dominions, the struggle between John and Arthur would be decided by how quickly they moved to secure the sinews of power: key castles, important towns, and treasuries. In this respect, one factor in particular counted in John's favour. According to Roger of Howden, Richard in his final days had named his brother as his heir. There is no way of knowing whether this was true, but it was certainly the case that those around the dying king – his household, comprised chiefly of Anglo-Norman barons – were firmly in favour of John. The same was true of his mother. Eleanor of Aquitaine was one of the few people who had been informed of the king's injury, and had rushed to Châlus to be with him when he died. Richard's condition had otherwise been kept secret, and messengers had raced to alert key personnel to an imminent change of leadership. William Marshal, for example, was staying in Rouen Castle because he had received orders to secure it three days before the king's death.[10]

The same messengers must have been sent speeding to locate John. The fact that he had fallen out with Richard just a few weeks earlier and withdrawn from his court may have made it difficult to do so. According to Howden he was in Normandy, but Howden may be giving us an airbrushed version of the truth, in keeping with his assertion that the two brothers had been reconciled before Richard met his end. Another source which provides a very detailed account of these days is *The Life of St Hugh*; its subject, the saintly Bishop Hugh of Lincoln, happened to be travelling to see Richard at this very moment, and was thus a key witness to the ensuing drama. According to Hugh's testimony, John was actually staying in Brittany at the time of Richard's death, keeping company with Arthur. If true (and there seems little reason to doubt it) this reinforces the suggestion that John may indeed have been plotting with his brother's enemies.[11]

Presumably John was informed in secret of his brother's fatal injury, made his excuses and departed. He must have been told to make straight for Chinon, the most important castle in Anjou, and the location of the county's treasury, for when he arrived there on the morning of 14 April his mother and his late brother's household were already waiting for him. They had come north from Châlus with Richard's body, and laid the dead king to rest at nearby Fontevraud alongside the bones of his father. John swore an oath to fulfil his brother's will faithfully – Richard had bequeathed a quarter of his treasure to his servants and the poor – and also promised to preserve the laws and customs of the people he would rule over, in return for which those present recognized him as his brother's successor.[12]

It remained to secure the rest of his dominions. From Chinon John headed north-west to the castle of Saumur, pausing en route at Fontevraud to visit his brother's tomb. By 18 April – Easter Sunday – he had reached the castle of Beaufort-en-Vallée, about fifteen miles east of Angers.[13]

At this point he realized he was in danger. While had been making his somewhat leisurely progress along the Loire, his enemies had been on the move. News of Richard's death must have broken at Arthur's court shortly after John's departure, and Constance of Brittany and the Breton nobles had immediately set out to advance Arthur's cause. By Easter Sunday they had already reached Angers, where they were met by a crowd of nobles from Anjou, Maine and Touraine, who all swore allegiance to Arthur as their new ruler.[14]

John was travelling with only a few attendants. Confrontation was out of the question; capture and indefinite imprisonment were a real possibility. His only hope was to outrun his enemies and reach Normandy before they caught up with him. On the morning of Easter Monday he set out at speed, covering fifty miles to reach Le Mans by nightfall. During his stay in the city, however, he realized that his situation had not improved. By now he must have known that Philip Augustus had invaded Normandy, seizing the town and county of Evreux, and was advancing in the direction of Le Mans. Fearing a trap, John stole away from the city in secret the next morning, disappearing into the pre-dawn darkness. In so doing he managed to escape the pincer just before it closed: a few hours later Arthur and his army attacked and occupied Le Mans, and a short while later they were joined there by the French king, who recognized Arthur's right to Anjou, Maine and Touraine in return for his homage. Apart from a handful of castles along the Loire Valley, Anjou had been lost.[15]

Normandy, fortunately, was far more welcoming. The Norman nobility can have had no great love or respect for John, remembering how he had demanded their allegiance when Richard was in captivity and then declined to help defend the duchy against Philip Augustus when that allegiance was refused. Nevertheless, as William Marshal had already recognized, in the ongoing struggle against the French king, John was now their only candidate. On 25 April he was invested as duke in Rouen Cathedral. The archbishop of Rouen, Walter de Coutances, who had opposed John's attempts to seize power in England, performed the ceremony, placing a coronet worked with golden roses on the new duke's head.[16]

England was evidently in John's thoughts at this time. News of Richard's death had arrived there by Easter and provoked outbreaks of opportunistic lawlessness. Ralph of Coggeshall reports that the magnates began 'ravaging like hungry wolves'. Such reports must have reached John in Normandy, for immediately after his investiture as duke he sent Hubert Walter and William Marshal across the Channel to help keep the peace in England until he could come there in person. For the moment, having secured the support of the Normans, John was inclined to attempt the recovery of lost ground in Anjou. Both the Bretons and Philip Augustus had since withdrawn from Le Mans, and John now returned to punish the city for its earlier disloyalty, tearing down its walls and castle and imprisoning many of its leading citizens. He may perhaps have met up with his mother, for Eleanor had embarked on a similar punitive expedition, leading Richard's mercenaries on a ravaging campaign through the Angevin countryside, demonstrating to local lords the downside of resisting Plantagenet power. Soon afterwards, however, they went their separate ways, Eleanor heading south to secure Aquitaine, John turning north in the direction of England.[17]

Hubert Walter and William Marshal may have found the situation in England worse than anticipated. The period between the death of one king and the coronation of his replacement was a legal vacuum that always tempted some men to settle old scores with violence, but this was something rather more serious. According to Roger of Howden, Hubert's and William's first move had been to administer a general oath of loyalty to John, but there was clearly widespread resistance. All those who held castles, says Howden, both barons and bishops, began strengthening them with men, provisions and arms. The king's lieutenants responded by calling a meeting to Northampton, summoning 'those persons of whom they had the greatest doubts'. It was an impressive list: five out of the seven men Howden names are earls, and he adds that there were many others. Most of those named had helped to crush John's rebellion against Richard and had been rewarded for their loyalty; no doubt they now feared that the sudden change in leadership would bring a sudden reversal in their fortunes. The archbishop and the Marshal, together with the justiciar, Geoffrey fitz Peter, pledged their word that John would give each man his due if they would preserve their fealty and keep the peace. Satisfied with the guarantees of these upright individuals, the magnates complied.[18]

John's advance guard must also have been charged with making preparations for his coronation, which was scheduled to take place at Ascension (27 May). John himself landed on the Sussex coast just two days beforehand and hurried to London. The fact that he left it until the very last minute to cross the Channel shows how concerned he must have been about leaving the Continent while his lands there were still being menaced. Ralph of Coggeshall says he departed from Normandy in secret, presumably in the hope of keeping his absence concealed from his enemies.[19]

John's coronation was not unusual in being hastily arranged. Ever since 1066, when the Normans had introduced the notion that the ceremony itself made a man a king, contenders for the English crown had held their coronations at the earliest opportunity. They were still solemn and magnificent affairs, with as much pageantry as possible. Ralph of Coggeshall says that John's coronation was conducted with great pomp, and Gervase of Canterbury says 'in great glory', but sadly there is little else in the way of contemporary description.[20] Like all coronations since the Conquest it took place in Westminster Abbey, where John was first required to swear a threefold oath, promising to protect and honour the Church, to abolish bad laws and replace them with good ones, and to do good justice to his subjects.[21] Afterwards came the king-making moment itself, in which he was anointed on various parts of his body with holy oil. Custom decreed that the oil poured on his head had to remain there for a full seven days, so for the whole week that followed John wore a special coif, with straps tied under his chin, to hold it in place. The new king was then dressed in royal robes and crowned, with a crown so heavy that two earls had to help support it on his head, before finally being seated on the throne while Mass was celebrated. Afterwards the king and his nobles walked the short distance to Westminster Hall for the coronation banquet. Twenty-one fat oxen from Worcestershire and 2,000 yards of table linen had been purchased for the occasion. William Marshal and Geoffrey fitz Peter, who had been officially recognized as earls that day by being girded with their swords of office, served at the king's table. Archbishop Hubert, who had performed the coronation service, was appointed as chancellor.[22]

The only discordant note during this otherwise harmonious fanfare was sounded by ambassadors sent by the king of Scots, William the Lion. Almost half a century earlier, when he was just a small boy, William had inherited the earldom of Northumbria (it came to him via his grandfather, David I, who had extorted it from King Stephen). Henry II had subsequently compelled William to return it, but the Scottish king had never abandoned the hope of getting it back. It had prompted his disastrous decision to join the rebellion against Henry in 1173, and had remained a bone of contention with Richard I. Now, with Richard dead and John struggling to secure his inheritance, he saw a golden opportunity. He would agree to recognize John, if John agreed to cede Northumbria. Messengers had already been sent to convey this offer to John before his return to England, but the regents in England had prevented them from crossing the Channel. And so the Scottish ambassadors had returned on the day of the coronation with the same urgent question: would the new king restore Northumbria, or would William be forced to take it?

John responded by inviting William to come and discuss the matter in person at Northampton in ten days' time, and duly set off in that direction soon after his coronation, visiting the shrines at St Albans and Bury St Edmunds on the way. But after waiting at Northampton for several days he was met by more Scottish ambassadors, who explained that their king would not be coming. Instead they delivered a more precise threat. Northumbria must be returned at once, or else William would take it by force. John was given forty days to make his mind up, during which time the king of Scots would be raising an army.

The new king of England had no intention of surrendering Northumbria or of waiting forty days in order to defend it. He too was busy raising an army, but it was to fight a far more formidable opponent. Delegating the problem of protecting northern England to William de Stuteville, John set out in the direction of the south coast, leaving the Scottish envoys trailing in his wake. On 20 June, less than four weeks since his arrival, he set sail from Shoreham, taking with him what Ralph of Coggeshall describes as 'a mighty English host'.[23]

Normandy seems not to have suffered from any new assaults during John's absence. It probably helped that on 23 May, just two days before he had left for England, the leading nobles of

Poitou, rallied by his mother, had launched an attack on Tours, where Arthur of Brittany was known to be staying. This was unsuccessful in that Arthur escaped, but it did succeed in drawing the fire of Philip Augustus, who was forced to send some of his troops south. When John landed at Dieppe with his great English army on 20 June, he found the situation encouraging. A few days later a multitude of Norman knights and infantry flocked to Rouen to join their ranks. For the same reason, the French king decided to put out peace feelers, and so a truce was agreed, set to last a little under two months.[24]

During this truce John spent much of his time visiting the towns and castles along Normandy's southern and eastern borders, no doubt shoring up their defences against future attack. He also set about strengthening his position by securing an impressive list of allies. In the last year of his life Richard had assembled a formidable coalition against Philip Augustus, wooing to his side most of the counts and dukes who were notionally subject to the French king. John now succeeded in confirming these alliances. On 13 August the count of Flanders did homage to him in Rouen, along with many others (fifteen counts in total, according to a local chronicler). All of them swore an oath against King Philip.[25]

Thus by the time the truce expired on 16 August John was in a very strong position with regard to his rival. On that day the two kings travelled to the border to discuss their differences, meeting on a stretch of the Seine between Les Andelys and Vernon that had become the norm for such conferences since the completion of Château Gaillard.[26] After two days of communicating through intermediaries, they at last came face to face. John, says Howden, asked why Philip held him in such hatred, asserting that he had never done him any harm. Philip replied that John had taken possession of Normandy and other territories without first obtaining the necessary permission; he should have come to Philip first and done homage. He then outlined the territorial settlement he had in mind. John was to hand over the whole of the Vexin to Philip, and to relinquish his claim to

Anjou, Maine and Touraine, which rightly belonged to Arthur.

John had no hesitation in rejecting these demands. Philip's view of his rights as overlord, John might have pointed out, was over-exalted. The kings of France had always liked to think of the Plantagenets as their vassals, and Henry II had encouraged this belief by having his sons do homage from time to time. As king of England, however, Henry had long resisted the suggestion that he should do homage in person. Only once, in 1183, had he done so, at a time when his bargaining power was weak. The very fact that the kings of France came to negotiate with their Plantagenet neighbours on the frontier of their respective territories, sometimes on islands in the middle of the Seine (or once, in Richard's case, shouting from a boat) indicates that, from the Plantagenet point of view at least, this was a relationship of equals. John had readily done homage to Philip in 1193, but then he had been a desperate rebel; he had no intention of repeating the performance now he was king of England.[27]

As for Philip's demand that John surrender Anjou, Maine and Touraine to Arthur, these territories sat at the centre of John's continental dominions. To cede them would be to rip the heart out of the Angevin Empire, severing communication between its northern and southern parts. Fortunately, John did not have to entertain such outrageous proposals. He still had his mighty English army, bolstered by the military support of Normandy, and he also had his impressive array of allies from elsewhere in France. On 18 August, as talks with Philip Augustus broke up without agreement, the count of Boulogne joined John's alliance. The English king, says Gervase of Canterbury, 'made up his mind to resist the French king like a man, and to fight manfully for the peace of his country'.[28]

And so hostilities resumed. Philip may have struck the first blow, augmenting his existing gains in south-east Normandy by seizing the castle at Conches, but it quickly became clear that the momentum was with John. In the second week of September he advanced from southern Normandy into Maine, drawing the French king south. Around the middle of the month, Philip besieged and destroyed the castle at Ballon, a few miles north of Le Mans.[29]

It was at this moment that John received an unexpected visit from William des Roches. William was one of the most powerful barons in Maine and Anjou, thanks to his marriage to a rich heiress some ten years earlier. Now in his mid-forties, he had a strong track record of loyalty to the Plantagenets, remaining with Henry II up to his death and accompanying Richard on crusade. In April 1199, however, he had decided to back Arthur rather than John. His reasons for doing so are unknown. He may have felt, like other Angevin nobles, that Arthur simply had the better claim. He must have been induced by a promise of increased power, for Arthur had immediately appointed him as seneschal of Anjou. But by September William had come to rue this decision. His specific reason, reported by several chroniclers, was Philip's behaviour at the siege of Ballon; William argued that the castle ought to have been handed over to Arthur, but the French king had haughtily dismissed his objections and burnt it to the ground. Behind this, his broader reason must surely have been that by September John was clearly winning the war. During the summer all the other powerful men in France had given him their backing, and he was now advancing confidently into Arthur's supposed area of authority. William must have feared that he was going to end up with nothing. And so, with the two armies not far apart, he secretly slipped away from Philip's side and came at night to John's camp. In the course of a personal interview with the king, he explained that he was ready to defect. But that was not all. He also assured John that, if he promised to act on his advice, he would arrange to bring in Arthur and his mother Constance. John's rival for power was ready to submit.[30]

John readily agreed. On 18 September he promised, in writing, to abide by whatever peace terms William arranged between himself and his 'very dear nephew, Arthur'. Then, emboldened by the prospect of success, he went on the offensive, surprising Philip Augustus as he was laying siege to the castle of Lavardin, twenty-five miles north-west of Le Mans.[31] Philip retreated into the city, but Le Mans, thanks to John's destruction of its walls and castle earlier in the year, was no longer defensible. With his enemies still in pursuit, the French king fled once again, this time withdrawing from Maine altogether. At some point before his departure he had agreed to place Arthur and his mother in the keeping of William des Roches, wrongly assuming that the seneschal of Anjou was still on his side. On 22 September William, who had been left in charge of Le Mans, welcomed John into the city and presented him with his nephew, just as he had promised. This was a moment of triumph. John, barely a fortnight into his campaign, had driven the king of France from the field, and – much more importantly – obtained the submission of Arthur.[32]

And yet it was only a fleeting moment, for within just a few hours John's victory was undone. As Roger of Howden explains, on the same day that Arthur submitted at Le Mans, he was warned that his uncle 'intended to take him and throw him in prison'. In the case of other rulers, such a warning would have been hard to believe. John, after all, had sworn to abide by the counsel of William des Roches, and had agreed (according to *The History of William Marshal*) that he, William and Arthur 'would all be good friends'; the letters issued by the king himself use phrases like 'firmly promised' and 'in good faith'. But John's catalogue of earlier betrayals clearly limited the value of such promises, and made rumours of impending treachery seem all too credible. The night after his submission, Arthur slipped away from his uncle's court, along with his mother and many others, and fled to Angers, which was still being held by his supporters. John, who had moved south to Chinon, rushed back to Le Mans, but the horse had already bolted. A week later he went south again, this time to Saumur, perhaps trying to intercept Arthur or prevent him moving eastward along the Loire, but if so without success. Arthur managed to travel from Angers to Tours, where he was received once more by Philip Augustus.[33]

Having let his nephew slip through his fingers, and with no other obvious enemies to fight, John returned to Normandy in the second week of October. Soon afterwards, at the urgings of a papal legate, both sides agreed to a truce that would last until early January. John must have been kicking himself at having so carelessly dropped his trump card. Ralph of Diceto commented that, in losing Arthur, the king had acted 'less than cautiously', and others appear to have arrived at similar negative conclusions. During the truce, many of the French nobles who had sworn oaths to fight with John took the cross and prepared to go on crusade. Had they been exasperated by his ineptitude, or perhaps shocked by his alleged plan to betray his nephew and throw him into prison? Whatever their reasons, by Christmas John's coalition against Philip Augustus had completely collapsed.[34]

This collapse was reflected in the peace terms that were agreed when the two kings met in January. In contrast to his determination not to give ground the previous year, John now made considerable territorial concessions, ceding to Philip all of the Vexin as well as all the towns and castles the French king had seized in south-east Normandy in the wake of Richard's death. Philip in return promised to stop supporting Arthur's claim, and induced Arthur himself to do the same; John was recognized as the rightful heir to Anjou, Maine and Touraine. Significantly, however, John accepted that he ought to do homage to Philip for these territories, as well as for Normandy, admitting the French king's superior lordship in a way that he and his ancestors had previously sought to resist. In recognition of this new dependency, he took the unprecedented step of promising to pay a relief of 20,000 marks.

Despite these substantial concessions, John may have thought that the deal he had achieved was a good one. He and Philip reportedly stood talking for a long time and embraced each other warmly. Others certainly thought it was a good deal, and welcomed the prospect of an end to seven years of almost continuous conflict. Ralph of Coggeshall commented that John 'was a lover of peace, who intended to live a tranquil life free from wars, understanding how many enemies of the kingdom he faced, and what great misfortunes had befallen his father and brothers and all the kingdom from such frequent wars'. Gervase of Canterbury was similarly pleased. By acting manfully, he thought, John had cowed his opponents, and 'by prudence more than war he had obtained peace everywhere'. But Gervase also noted that not everyone was impressed by the king's performance. Some people, 'malevolent and envious', were calling him 'Soft-sword'. In other words, the monks commended John's peace; the military men thought he ought to have put up more of a fight.[35]

The peace drawn up in January 1200 was for the moment agreed only in principle. To seal it permanently, and to give Philip's territorial gains the appearance of a freely conceded gift, there was to be a royal wedding. Philip's eldest son Louis would marry John's niece, Blanche – the daughter of his sister Eleanor and her husband, Alfonso VIII of Castile. This meant that the bride would have to be fetched from Spain, and so a further five-month truce was put in place to enable this. Eleanor of Aquitaine, by this point in her mid-seventies, set out across the Pyrenees to collect her granddaughter.[36]

John in the meantime crossed the Channel to England, arriving in Portsmouth at the end of February. To the dismay of Ralph of Coggeshall, he immediately proved that peace could be as expensive as war by imposing a heavy tax to raise his 20,000-mark relief. As Coggeshall explained, this new demand, coming as it did after the scutage to finance the previous year's military campaign, 'very much weakened the people of the land'. John also intended during this visit to deal with the king of Scots. Despite his earlier threats, William the Lion had not raised an army or attempted to take Northumbria. John summoned him to York and travelled there in expectation of a meeting at the end of March. By this stage, however, William's courage had completely deserted him. The confrontational stance he had adopted in 1199 had been based on the assumption that the new king of England would be distracted by his problems on the Continent; there is some evidence to suggest he was acting in concert with Philip Augustus. But now that John and Philip had all but settled their differences, William was isolated, and must have feared retribution. Claiming that John's assurance of safe conduct was inadequate, he again declined to appear.[37]

The Scottish king's repeated failure to present himself must have angered John, but not as much as the appearance at York of several Cistercian abbots, who had been summoned to the city to discuss their contribution to the recent tax. The Cistercians had always been exempt from taxation, but when they pointed this out and refused to pay, the king exploded. In 'anger and fury', according to Ralph of Coggeshall, he ordered his sheriffs to persecute the Cistercians by all possible means, and to take no action against those who harmed them. The abbots complained about these 'cruel edicts' to the archbishop of Canterbury, who in turn 'freely rebuked the king for such great cruelty, denouncing him as a persecutor of the holy Church'. But despite this and subsequent attempts to placate him, John refused to be pacified, and sailed for Normandy at the end of April, 'breathing fire and slaughter against the followers of Christ'.[38]

By the time John recrossed the Channel, his mother had returned from her trip to Spain, bringing with her the bride-to-be, Blanche of Castile. Eleanor was too exhausted to travel any further than Bordeaux, so it fell to the city's archbishop to escort Blanche on the final stage of her journey to Normandy, where she was at last delivered to her waiting uncle. On 18 May John and Philip met at the border and the terms they had agreed in January were confirmed. Four days later, on an island in the middle of the Seine called Le Goulet, the peace was sealed. John did homage to Philip for his continental possessions, Arthur did homage to John for Brittany, and Blanche was married to Philip's son, Louis. The war of succession to the Angevin Empire was finally over.[39]

A fortnight after the peace was sealed, John set out south, to take possession of those territories that had spent the previous year resisting him: Maine, Anjou and Touraine. In expectation of continued resistance, he took no chances and advanced at the head of a large army, passing in turn through the cities of Le Mans, Angers and Tours. At Angers he stayed for four nights and took 150 hostages.[40]

In July he moved further south into Aquitaine. The great southern duchy had been secured for him the previous year by his mother, but only by making generous concessions to its leading nobles, granting them lands and castles in order to persuade them to stay loyal. Such was the way Aquitaine had to be governed, for ducal authority there had always been weak. Like his predecessors, John had little land of his own in the duchy and very few castles. To rule effectively it was necessary to work with the local aristocracy, sometimes appeasing them, sometimes playing them off against each other. Politics were thus naturally fractious, and rebellions more frequent than elsewhere in the Angevin Empire. It had been in Aquitaine that Richard had met his end, trying to suppress the rebellion of the viscount of Limoges and the count of Angoulême. As John prepared to advance into the duchy, he summoned both these men to come and do homage to him at Lusignan on 5 July. The choice of location was significant: the lord of Lusignan, Hugh le Brun, had been a rival of the count of Angoulême for many years, but lately they had agreed to bury the hatchet, and Hugh had agreed to marry the count's only daughter and heir.[41]

John had been giving much thought to his own marriage in recent months. As we have seen, his wedding to Isabella of Gloucester in 1189 was probably a forced affair, performed at Richard's insistence. With Richard gone, John was at last free to please himself. His intention to divorce Isabella must have been apparent from the very start of his reign, for she was not crowned with him in May 1199, and later that year he persuaded the bishops of Normandy to declare their marriage void. Other churchmen disapproved. The dean of St Paul's, Ralph of Diceto, thought that John had acted 'on the advice of evil men', and claimed that the king's actions had angered the pope. But John had good political reasons for wanting a divorce at this point, for he was recruiting allies against Philip Augustus, and was hoping to marry the daughter of the king of Portugal. In January 1200 Portuguese ambassadors had been received at his court.[42]

Whether John was still thinking about a Portuguese marriage

by the summer of 1200 is altogether more doubtful. His first reported act on reaching Aquitaine was to ask the local bishops to confirm his divorce, and on 10 July he did send ambassadors to Portugal. But the suspicion is that this last act was a smoke-screen to conceal his real intentions, for by this stage the king was secretly planning to marry elsewhere. In late July and early August, as he toured the south of the duchy, shock news arrived at court: the count of Angoulême had abducted his daughter from the custody of her fiancé, Hugh de Lusignan. According to *The History of William Marshal*, Hugh was travelling with John's court, and departed in anger, knowing that this was part of a plot. And he was undoubtedly right: on 24 August, John came to Angoulême and married the girl himself.[43]

According to Roger of Howden, the motivation was 'affection': the king had simply taken a fancy to the count's daughter and acted on impulse. This is, of course, possible, but not very likely. John's new wife – who, like his old wife, was named Isabella – was very young. Although he subsequently persuaded half a dozen bishops to attest that their union was legitimate, she may have been under the minimum age set by the Church, which was twelve; had she been any older, it is difficult to explain why she had not already been married to her betrothed, Hugh de Lusignan.[44]

The more likely (and, indeed, more charitable) explanation is that John married Isabella for political reasons. In 1200 Hugh de Lusignan was a man who was growing too powerful for comfort. One factor, for example, which had for a long time kept him and the count of Angoulême in check was their competition for the county of La Marche. But in the wake of Richard's death Hugh had obtained La Marche from Eleanor of Aquitaine (in one account, by kidnapping the queen and extorting it from her); at the start of 1200, John had been obliged to recognize Hugh's possession of the county as a fait accompli. Had his marriage to Isabella gone ahead as planned, Hugh would also have been set to inherit all of Angoulême. Together, these new acquisitions would have placed him in control of a huge power bloc, covering an area greater than Normandy, and cutting communication between the northern and southern parts of the Angevin Empire. By marrying Isabella, John had nipped this prospect in the bud, and secured Angoulême for himself. From a strategic point of view, this was a masterstroke.[45]

From a political point of view it was a disaster. 'This did not have a favourable outcome,' says *The History of William Marshal*, 'for the count of La Marche [i.e. Hugh de Lusignan] and his men left with anger in their hearts. They did not feel it was right that the girl had been abducted.' Not for the first time, John had sought to achieve desirable ends by resorting to under-hand methods, only to find that his scheme had backfired. It was perhaps unlikely that Hugh would have responded favourably to any candid, upfront suggestions that he break off an engagement which promised to increase his power so substantially, but in any case John made no attempt to placate him or offer anything by way of compensation. According to two contemporaries, the idea of marrying Isabella had been planted in the king's head by Philip Augustus. If that really was the case, then John ought to have been more circumspect, for the resulting ill will worked greatly to the French king's advantage.[46]

As soon as his wedding had been celebrated, John and Isabella set out in the direction of England. In early October they crossed the Channel and on 8 October they were both crowned in Westminster Abbey. (Ralph of Coggeshall, recording the event, charitably remarked that the new queen looked 'about twelve'.) Immediately after the ceremony, John summoned the king of Scots for a third time, sending a powerful delegation (one bishop, three earls and four barons) to give him the desired safe conduct. William must have realized he could put the matter off no longer; regardless of his claim to Northumbria, he held lands from the English king that he could not expect to retain if he failed to acknowledge John as his lord. The two kings met in Lincoln on 21 November. The following day, on top of a lofty hill outside the city, surrounded by a vast crowd of people from England, Scotland and Normandy, William did homage to John, kneeling before him and swearing eternal fidelity. William then raised the subject of Northumbria but discovered that, alas, John did not think much of his claim. The matter was postponed.[47]

A few days later, John also settled his row with the Cistercians. He had returned to England in no mood for compromise – on the day of Isabella's coronation he had increased their persecution by issuing more 'cruel edicts' – but at length his heart softened. The Cistercian abbots had gathered in Lincoln to seek his mercy at the suggestion of the archbishop of Canterbury who, after several days of patient cajoling, persuaded the king to grant them an audience. They fell down at his feet and begged forgiveness, and he, to their surprise, responded in kind, tearfully cancelling his earlier oppressions and promising in future to be their protector. He also proclaimed his wish to build a new Cistercian monastery for the good of his soul and the souls of his parents, where he intended one day to be buried.[48]

Thus, by Christmas, which was spent at Guildford, John could feel that all his major problems had been solved. His war against Philip Augustus and Arthur of Brittany was over, his succession to the Angevin Empire secure. His superiority to the king of Scots had been ritually established, and his rift with the Cistercians healed. He had divorced his older, unwanted first wife, and replaced her with a young, attractive and politically useful new queen. Soon into the new year 1201 he and Isabella set out on a tour of northern England.[49]

But in Poitou, the king's success was starting to unravel, precisely because of his second marriage. In the early months of 1201 Hugh de Lusignan, still chafing at his humiliation, rebelled against John's authority and began attacking the king's castles in Aquitaine. He was joined by his uncle, Geoffrey de Lusignan, a former crusader famous for his military prowess, and many other men besides. According to the Anonymous of Béthune, the whole nobility of Poitou was up in arms on account of what they regarded as the shabby treatment of Hugh. Eleanor of Aquitaine, who had retired to spend her final days at Fontevraud, sent panicked letters to her son in England, spelling out his deteriorating fortunes.[50]

John, returning from his tour of the north, responded in the early spring, ordering his officials to seize the county of La Marche from Hugh de Lusignan. He also struck at Hugh's brother, Ralph, who held the county of Eu in Normandy, instructing his deputies in the duchy to seize all Ralph's territories. This was more controversial, because Ralph had seemingly not participated in his brother's rebellion; indeed, according to one chronicler, he was in John's service in England when the king ordered the attack on his estates. John was apparently bent on crushing the entire Lusignan clan, and not paying much attention to individual culpability. Shortly after Easter he ordered his English nobles to muster at Portsmouth in May, ready to engage his continental enemies.[51]

John's decision to wage indiscriminate war against Hugh and his family would have mattered less had he not recognized Philip Augustus as his overlord the previous year. As it was, his enemies were able to complain to the French king that they were being unjustly persecuted. Philip responded by acting as peacemaker, persuading the Lusignans to stop their attacks in Poitou, and arranging to meet John on the Norman–French border. The two kings renewed their commitment to the peace they had sealed twelve months earlier, and John ordered the restoration of Ralph de Lusignan's estates. Afterwards John accompanied Philip to Paris, where he was lodged in the royal palace and entertained lavishly (though laughed at after his departure, when it was discovered his men had drunk all the bad wines and left the good ones). In the course of this visit, John promised to give the Lusignans justice, and Philip agreed not to press the matter further.[52]

It soon became apparent, however, that John had a particularly rough form of justice in mind. Once he had returned to his own lands, he charged the Lusignans with treachery, and challenged them to a judicial duel. There was nothing illegal in this, but it was a decidedly old-fashioned way to proceed in an age that was increasingly reliant on settling such matters in court. John, moreover, set about ensuring his victory by recruiting the best fighting men he could find across all his dominions to act as his champions. This was effectively war by other means. Unsurprisingly the Lusignans refused to answer his summons, saying that they would only accept trial by their peers, and once again appealed to Philip Augustus.[53]

Philip intervened once more, and insisted that the Lusignans be given a fair hearing. John agreed, but began dragging his heels, refusing to set a date or to grant the Lusignans safe conduct. In the autumn Philip tried to apply some pressure, demanding that John guarantee his word by handing over the castles of Falaise, Arques and Château Gaillard. But since these were three of the most important fortresses in Normandy, John naturally refused, sending the archbishop of Canterbury to the French king's court to tender his excuses.[54]

By the start of 1202 patience was wearing thin on both sides. A conference was arranged for 25 March between the two kings, but they did not meet in person, communicating only through proxies. Philip insisted that John should come to Paris and stand trial for his contempt; John, perhaps belatedly realizing the negative connotations of his trip to Paris the previous year, countered that the dukes of Normandy had always been accustomed to meet the kings of France at the frontier. John was not being summoned as the duke of Normandy, replied Philip, but as the duke of Aquitaine and count of Anjou, territories for which he had lately done homage. And so their arguments went on from day to day, says Ralph of Coggeshall, and their hostility began to increase. The meeting apparently concluded with a climbdown by John, who promised to appear in Paris on 28 April to answer for his contempt, and to surrender two castles as security. But in the event he did neither, and so on that date Philip's court found against him. John was declared to be a contumacious vassal, and all his lands were deemed forfeit.[55]

At once Philip set about putting the sentence into effect, launching an attack on Normandy and taking Boutavant, one of the two castles John had promised as security, which he then razed to the ground. The French king had evidently been preparing his assault for many weeks in advance, for in the month that followed many other fortresses along the Norman border also fell. John lurked nearby but put up no resistance; only when Philip moved to besiege the castle at Radepont, ten miles south-east of Rouen, did his opponent move towards him, forcing him into a temporary retreat.[56]

By this point, the French king was ready to open up another front, using a pawn that had been out of play for over a year. In early July he had knighted Arthur of Brittany and betrothed him to his infant daughter, Mary. At the same time, he had invested Arthur with Anjou, Maine, Touraine and Aquitaine – all the territories that John was deemed to have forfeited, except Normandy, which Philip was determined to keep for himself. Arthur was now fifteen years of age, and his knighting signified that he was considered old enough to fight for his inheritance. The French king immediately sent him south with 200 knights to join forces with the Lusignans, to escalate the war against John in Aquitaine.[57]

When Arthur and his army met up with the Lusignans and their supporters in Tours towards the end of July, they had exciting news. Eleanor of Aquitaine, who was still regarded as one of the most important pieces on the board, had left Fontevraud, where she would obviously have been an easy target, and was heading in the direction of Poitiers. This was too good an opportunity to miss. Ignoring Arthur's suggestion that they wait for the troops he had summoned from Brittany, they set off at once, and caught up with Eleanor at Mirebeau, fifteen miles north of Poitiers. The queen and her household retreated into the castle, but managed to dispatch a messenger to her son, warning him that she was in imminent danger of being taken prisoner.[58]

John, knowing that Arthur had set out to meet the Lusignans, had already started to head in the same direction. He was at Le Mans when his mother's messenger reached him on 30 July. The situation must have seemed hopeless, for Mirebeau and Le Mans are almost a hundred miles apart, but John nevertheless set off at once. Taking a detachment of his army, he rode south at a gallop, covering the whole distance in under forty-eight hours.[59]

At dawn on 1 August the king and his knights fell upon their unsuspecting enemies. Arthur and the Lusignans had already taken the town of Mirebeau and occupied the outer ward of the castle, forcing Eleanor and her followers to retreat into the keep. They were enjoying a leisurely breakfast – Geoffrey de Lusignan was having pigeons – when the king's men rushed into the town, storming the one gate that had not been blocked. Fierce fighting followed in the streets – 'many a helmet was staved in', says *The History of William Marshal* – but in a short while John's troops were completely victorious. All of those who had been besieging his mother were taken prisoner, including Hugh de Lusignan, Geoffrey de Lusignan, and – most importantly – Arthur. Altogether, the king calculated that he and his men had captured half a dozen barons, 200 knights and innumerable infantry. It was a greater and more decisive victory than had ever been won by his father or brother. John sent a jubilant letter to his regents in England, describing his triumph in detail, and concluding with the words 'God be praised for our happy success!'[60]

7

King versus Pope

1207–1208

John had returned to England in December 1206 buoyed by the achievements of that year's continental campaign. The last Castilian garrisons had been driven from Aquitaine, and much booty had reportedly been captured; he had secured his hold on his wife's county of Angoulême and recovered the southern part of Poitou. Tantalizingly, he had led a sortie north into Anjou, and for a week had held court in Angers, his family's ancestral seat. Such was the good progress that the king and his magnates were able to celebrate during the Christmas immediately after his return.[1]

And yet John's success in 1206 merely emphasized how much work still needed to be done. His newly won laurels, whilst pleasing, were little ones, and he certainly could not afford to rest on them during the two-year truce that was now in place. It had taken him months of politicking and arm-twisting to raise an army to take to Poitou and the money to sustain it. If he was going to reconquer Normandy, Maine and Anjou, he was going to need to field much larger forces for a much longer period, and that would mean raising a great deal more cash. After John's loss of Normandy in 1204 it is possible to detect a new note of urgency in his government of England; from the start of 1207 it rose to an even sharper pitch.[2]

The king's first thought was to seek financial assistance from the clergy. The English Church was still leaderless in December 1206, because the controversy over who should be archbishop of Canterbury had continued. One year earlier, as we've seen, John had browbeaten the monks of Canterbury into accepting his preferred candidate, John de Gray, the bishop of Norwich, on learning that some of them had secretly elected one of their own number. But in May 1206, on the eve of his departure for Poitou, the king had received disappointing news from Rome. The pope, confronted by the conflicting claims and counterclaims from both sides, and perturbed by reports of royal coercion, had cancelled Gray's election and announced he would review the matter himself. A decision had been expected in the autumn, but so far there had been no news.[3]

At the start of 1207 John paid a short visit to Canterbury, perhaps rehearsing his case for cash with the local clergy. A few days later he travelled to London to meet a great council of magnates and prelates that had been summoned to assemble on 8 January, and put to them his plan. What he wanted, he explained to the bishops and abbots, was their permission to take a fixed portion of the income of every beneficed clergyman in the country. The bishops and abbots refused, possibly on the grounds that they had not been given time enough to consult, or that not enough of them were present; the king, after all, had not yet been back in the country for a month, so the council must have been called at short notice. A second council was summoned to meet in Oxford in four weeks' time.

The Oxford council was certainly well attended. Our best-informed source, the annalist at Waverley Abbey in Surrey, reports 'an infinite multitude of prelates and magnates'. When the demand for cash was put to the clergy for a second time, their answer was more decisive. 'The English Church', they replied, 'could by no means submit to a demand which had never been heard of in all previous ages.' According to the Waverley annalist, John then relented, 'having taken wiser counsel'.[4]

In fact, the king and his counsellors had in the meantime come up with an even more ambitious plan to tax everyone in the country, clergy and laity, from the highest earl or bishop to the poorest parson or peasant. This was not wholly unprecedented, but such general taxes were still sufficiently rare to be extremely controversial. The kings of Anglo-Saxon England had levied a tax known as the geld (or Danegeld, because they used it to pay off the Vikings and recruit Danish mercenaries), and it had continued to be levied after the Norman Conquest. But the geld had been eroded by exemptions. The Norman nobility had refused to pay it, and in consequence its yield had shrunk to the point at which it was outweighed by the unpopularity of collecting it. Henry II had levied it for the last time in 1162. Since then, general taxes had been sought only in extraordinary circumstances, and only with the consent of a great council. Henry had permitted the Church to collect three aids for the Holy Land, culminating in the Saladin Tithe of 1188, which demanded ten per cent of everyone's goods and revenue. A similar levy had been imposed by Richard I's regents in 1193 to raise his £100,000 ransom, the rate on that occasion set at an eye-watering twenty-five per cent. This tax must go a long way to explaining why chroniclers complained about the unheard-of amounts of money that were extracted during Richard's reign; it would also explain why, when the king tried to get a similar tax to fight Philip Augustus in 1197, he was refused. Taxation was regarded as tantamount to robbery, only to be granted in times of truly exceptional need.[5]

Seven years into his reign, John had already asked for taxes on two previous occasions. In 1200, he had sought an aid to pay his relief to Philip Augustus for inheriting the duchy of Normandy. Its yield is unknown, but was probably not great. Like the geld, it was levied on units of land rather than actual income, and as such failed to tap the country's true wealth. It was nevertheless unpopular. The Cistercians, as we have seen, protested against paying it and suffered months of persecution before finally winning their point. With altogether less success the king's half-brother, Archbishop Geoffrey of York, refused to allow his lands to be assessed and was deprived of them as a result until he relented. In 1203 John had imposed another tax, this time on the more dubious grounds that his military tenants in England had failed to support him in the fight for Normandy. This time the assessment was based on wealth, but only on revenues, not on goods. The scant impact it made on both royal records and contemporary chroniclers suggest it may have been even less successful, raising somewhere in the region of £7,000.[6]

At Oxford in February 1207 John demanded something far more ambitious: a tax to be assessed on both the income and the goods of every man. To justify this demand he referred to 'the defence of our realm and the recovery of our right'. Considering that Richard had failed to obtain consent to a similar demand during a time of war, John's attempt to get a tax at the start of a two-year truce was ambitious, even audacious. And yet, remarkably, the request was approved by the assembled magnates and prelates. The rate, probably negotiated, was set at one shilling in every mark, which equates to 7.5 per cent. Because a mark was worth just over thirteen shillings (13s 4d), contemporaries referred to it as the Thirteenth. According to the royal writ ordering the collection, it had been granted 'by common counsel, and with the assent of our council at Oxford'. According to Roger of Wendover, the king's request 'caused great murmuring among all, though they dared not contradict it'.[7]

The measures put in place to raise the tax were elaborate and unremitting. Assessment was made by specially appointed justices, who visited every town and parish within their particular county. Fourteen men, for example, were charged with the task in Lincolnshire. In each district, every local man had to appear before them and swear to the value of his rents and moveable goods; the justices made a record of the amount of tax due, which was then passed to the sheriff for collection. Penalties for evasion were harsh: those found guilty of making false declarations, or otherwise concealing their wealth, were to be cast into prison and have all their goods confiscated for the king's use.[8]

One magnate, in fact, did dare to contradict the demand made during the Oxford council. Archbishop Geoffrey of York, who had been dispossessed for opposing the tax of 1200, strongly

objected to the new demand of 1207 and excommunicated the
men who tried to levy it within his archdiocese. As on the
previous occasion, John reacted by seizing his half-brother's lands
and goods, prompting Geoffrey to appear before him. Perhaps
remembering the successful histrionics of the Cistercian abbots
in 1200, the archbishop fell at the king's feet to appeal for grace.
John, however, simply responded in kind, falling at Geoffrey's
feet, laughing and jeering, saying 'Look, my lord archbishop,
even as you do, so do I!' Unable to gain redress, Geoffrey appealed
to the pope and went into exile.[9]

By this point, the pope was not high on John's list of favourite
people. Early in 1207, probably around the time of the Oxford
council, news had arrived in England about the outcome of the
Canterbury dispute. The pope, Innocent III, had finally heard
the case in December. At his request fifteen Canterbury monks
had come to Rome, as well as representatives of the English
bishops and the king. Innocent had begun by rejecting the bishops'
claim to have a say in the election of a new archbishop, confirming
that this right belonged exclusively to the monks. This was a
blow for John's cause, but when the pope called upon the monks
to make their choice, he found that they were divided among
themselves, some still supporting their sub-prior, Reginald, others
now favouring the king's nominee, John de Gray. At this point
Innocent intervened. Since they could not agree on either of the
existing candidates, he proposed – or imposed, according to some
sources – a third. The man the pope had in mind was Stephen
Langton, a scholar of international reputation, lately summoned
from Paris to Rome to become a cardinal, but by birth an
Englishman who had begun his clerical career in York. The king's
representatives objected to this development, but were powerless
to prevent it going forward. The monks, probably after experiencing a certain amount of papal pressure, unanimously elected
Langton. A few days before Christmas, Innocent wrote to John
to inform him of the good news.[10]

The king was furious – 'exceedingly enraged', according to

Roger of Wendover, 'as much at the promotion of Stephen Langton as at the annulment of the election of the bishop of Norwich'. In response, he sent a hot-tempered letter back to the pope, making no attempt to disguise his displeasure. It was disgraceful, he said, that Innocent had cancelled John de Gray's election and appointed 'a man altogether unknown to him, who had been familiar for a long time with his declared enemies in the kingdom of France'. Moreover, apart from his particular objection to Langton, there was the general principle at stake, namely that the king of England ought to have a say in the appointment of the archbishop of Canterbury; between them, the pope and the monks of Canterbury had conspired to deny John that right. Reminding Innocent that England contributed more funds to the papal treasury than any other country north of the Alps, the king vowed that he would defend the rights of his Crown to the death, and declared he would not be deterred from his intention of making John de Gray his next archbishop. For good measure, he concluded with an outright threat, saying that he would cut all communication between England and Rome if the pope did not fall in line with his wishes.[11]

John's letter to Innocent was probably dispatched around mid-April, at which point the king was at Lambeth. For most of the rest of the spring, while contemplating his response, the king had been travelling between his hunting lodges in southern and midland England. Like almost all medieval monarchs, John was a keen huntsman. Hunting was the main leisure activity of the medieval upper classes: it kept them in shape; it enabled them to practise their horsemanship and hone their use of weapons; it also put food on the table. Even so, contemporary comment suggests that John was keener than most. The poet Bertran de Born contrasted the king's passion for 'pointers, greyhounds and hawks' with his apparent lack of martial prowess, while the Anonymous of Béthune said that he 'haunted woods and streams and greatly delighted in the pleasure of them'. John was not a great castle-builder, but his one original foundation was the tower he built at Odiham in Hampshire, substantial remains of which still survive. Begun in the first half of 1207, it was constructed, according to the Anonymous of Béthune, so the king could disport himself in the surrounding forests.[12]

The royal forest in which John hunted was not simply a reserve set aside for the king's enjoyment. It was also a highly developed sub-branch of government, almost a state within the state. The concept of a royal forest, governed by its own law, had been introduced to England by William the Conqueror. (The word 'forest', introduced at the same time, derives from the Latin *foris*, meaning 'outside' or 'apart'.) Forest law was extremely harsh. The penalty for taking a deer, established by the Conqueror, was blinding. It was also entirely arbitrary. 'The whole organization of the forests,' wrote Henry II's treasurer, Ralph fitz Nigel, 'and the punishment, financial and corporal, of forest offences, is outside the jurisdiction of the other courts, and solely dependent on the decision of the king, or of some officer specially appointed by him … What is done in accordance with forest law is not called "just" without qualification, but "just, according to the forest law".'[13]

The simple solution, one might conclude, was to stay out of the royal forest; but for many people that was not an option. What had started after the Conquest as a royal hunting preserve had been massively extended during the twelfth century, chiefly by Henry II. Even as he was making the common law more accessible to his subjects, Henry was in this way extending his arbitrary power over them. By the end of his reign, the jurisdiction known as 'the Forest' did not apply only to the wooded or wasteland areas used for hunting, but to almost a third of all England. Land of any kind, arable or pasture, could be forest. Villages could be forest. All of Essex was forest.

Although Henry's love of hunting was almost as famous as that of his favourite son, he had not extended the scope of the Forest merely to extend his hunting rights; he had done so for financial gain. While savage corporal punishments could still be dished out – Richard I had increased the penalty for taking a deer to the loss of eyes *and* testicles – it was increasingly common for offenders to face fines. The forests were policed by a range of officials – foresters, verderers, regarders – ever vigilant for infringements, all under the ultimate control of the chief forester. During John's reign the chief forester was Hugh de Neville. Appointed by Richard in 1198, Hugh struck up a close working relationship with his new master after John's accession. Indeed, he became one of the king's most intimate companions, to judge from financial records that show the two of them gambling together from time to time.[14]

John's initial policy towards the Forest had been to raise money by selling exemptions, allowing men to turn forest land into arable (assarting) or simply declaring that certain areas were to be 'disafforested'. Hugh de Neville had been given a free hand to do this in 1203, when the king was in Normandy and in desperate need of ready cash, and extensive disafforestation had taken place the following year. But after his return to England in 1206, John changed tack, and decided it was time to exploit the Forest more efficiently without further diminishing its extent. Fines were raised from the Forest by periodically dispatching special itinerant justices, much like the regular justices the king sent round the country to hear common-law cases. There had been no such visitation, or eyre, since 1198, when Hugh de Neville had conducted one at the start of his term of office. But in the spring of 1207, while John was disporting himself in the forests of Hampshire, Northamptonshire and Dorset, a new eyre was launched by Hugh and his associates. They began in Cornwall, Devon, Hampshire, Northumberland, Rutland and Surrey. For the men of Cornwall this was a surprise, since in 1204 they had collectively given 2,200 marks and twenty palfreys to have their county disafforested. Hugh de Neville seems to have interpreted this as a temporary respite, for the eyre in Cornwall went ahead as normal and raised £325 in fines.[15]

The nature of the fines is recorded on the rolls of the Exchequer. Men were fined for hunting without the king's permission, or for attacking royal foresters. The foresters themselves were fined for laxity in carrying out their duties. A woman in Nottinghamshire paid 100 marks to recover land that had been confiscated because she had made a ditch without permission. The wide variety of offences was nothing new, but the eyre launched in 1207 was unquestionably more searching and more punitive than its predecessors. The total raised by Neville's previous eyre – which ran from 1198 to 1201, and was described by Roger of Howden as 'a torment to the men of the kingdom' – was £3,700. By the time the eyre launched in 1207 had finally run its course, it had raised £8,700.[16]

On 23 June 1207 John visited Odiham, either to initiate the building of his new castle there or to inspect its early progress. It must have been around this time that he received letters from Pope Innocent, sent from Rome four weeks earlier.[17]

The pope was not happy. He had not liked the tone of John's response. ('We wrote to you meekly and kindly, requesting and exhorting, but you wrote back to us insolently and impudently, as though threatening and expostulating.') Nor did he think much of the king's objections to the newly elected archbishop of Canterbury. John's claim that Stephen Langton had lived among his enemies and was 'unknown' to him was rejected as 'paltry'. If that really was the case, asked the pope, why had John written to Langton congratulating him on his promotion to the cardinalate? Innocent was similarly dismissive of the king's complaint about the lack of royal consent. Regardless of the procedural irregularities alleged by John's envoys, the fact was that the pope had plenary authority in this matter. Nothing could now impede Langton's advancement, and the king should not suppose otherwise. Matching threat with threat, Innocent concluded by warning John not 'to fight against God and the Church in this cause for which St Thomas [Becket], that glorious martyr and archbishop, recently shed his blood'.[18]

This letter gives us some insight into the character and motivations of Innocent III. Elected in January 1198, he had come to the papal throne at an exceptionally young age. His predecessors in recent decades had all been old men, appointed in their sixties, seventies and eighties, and thus had served for only a few years before their deaths. Innocent by contrast was thirty-seven or thirty-eight at the time of his election – three or four years younger than Richard I, whose rule had briefly overlapped with his own, and only six or seven years older than John. His early appointment to the most senior role in the Church gives some indication of how highly others thought of his abilities. A distinguished lawyer as well as an accomplished theologian, he was brilliant, quick-witted and abrasive, and came to power determined to assert papal authority to the full. The papacy had been asserting its supremacy on spiritual matters since the mid-eleventh century, at which point it had embraced the ideals of an earlier monastic reform movement. No pope, however, had pushed papal supremacy as hard as Innocent. He was, in his own words, 'less than God, but greater than Man, judge of all men and judged by none'. Having appointed Langton, he explained in his letter, 'we could not desist without loss of reputation or peril to our conscience'. Innocent was not a man for compromise.[19]

But nor was John. Aside from an Angevin temperament which made it unlikely that the king would back down, there was a clash of principles. The problem with Innocent's response was that it did not consider (or did not consider important) that, for John to desist, he would suffer a loss of reputation, and even peril to his own conscience. Part of the sacred oath that the king had sworn at his coronation was a promise, introduced by Henry II, to safeguard the rights of the Crown, and one of those rights was a say in the appointment of bishops.[20]

But by the time John received this letter, Innocent had already acted. On 17 June, without waiting for any further response from England, the pope personally consecrated Langton in the Italian city of Viterbo, fifty miles north of Rome. If his envoys travelled at lightning speed, it is just possible that news of this could have reached the king by 11 July. Equally there was enough in Innocent's letter for John to realize that this outcome was inevitable. Either way, on that date the king reacted, proclaiming that anyone who acknowledged Langton as archbishop would be considered a public enemy, and ordering two knights – Fulk de Cantilupe and Reginald of Cornhill, the sheriff of Kent – to expel the monks of Canterbury from England. Four days later these men, accompanied by a band of armed attendants, carried out their task. According to Wendover they entered the monastery with drawn swords, calling the monks traitors to the king and swearing that they would burn the monastery down if its occupants did not leave immediately. Thirteen monks lying in the infirmary were too sick to move, but the remaining sixty-four left at once, fleeing across the Channel to Flanders, where they found refuge at the abbey of St Bertin.[21]

John was back in Lambeth when he issued these orders, but by the time they were carried out he was en route to Winchester, perhaps to visit his queen, who was resident in Winchester Castle during the latter part of the year. The king's relationship with Isabella, the girl he had married seven summers earlier, is almost completely obscure. He was at least twenty years her senior, so their interests are unlikely to have overlapped, to begin with at any rate. After her coronation in October 1200 John had treated Isabella like the child she was, sometimes taking her with him on his travels, other times leaving her to stay at a favourite royal residence such as Marlborough, but certainly not entrusting her with any political power, and not even any land. This meant she was entirely reliant on the king's handouts, and royal financial records show she received a steady stream of necessities and luxury items. One of the men particularly concerned with attending to her needs was Reginald of Cornhill, the aforementioned sheriff of Kent. In 1207 he sent her, among other things, a gilded saddle and harness, three different-coloured hoods, a hundred yards of fine linen, two tablecloths, four towels, half an otter skin and a belt. Other entries show Isabella received clothes and equipment for her chaplains and payment for the keepers of her greyhounds.[22]

The financial records also suggest that, in one respect, the queen's domestic arrangements may have been unusual, in that she seems to have been lodged, at least for some of the time, in the same place as John's ex-wife. After their divorce in 1200 the king had continued to maintain Isabella of Gloucester, supplying her with goods and money on a scale that almost rivalled that of her replacement. Winchester Castle seems to have been her chief residence, and in 1205 and 1206 the expenses of the two Isabellas were recorded as if they were staying together under the same roof.

What this signifies about John's relationship with the two women is anyone's guess. It would take a considerable imaginative leap to suggest that he was keeping his former wife, now in her mid-forties, as a mistress, given that he had apparently not wanted to marry her in the first place. At the same time, the king's lack of legitimate children by 1207 suggests that he may not have been sleeping with his teenage queen, despite Wendover's scurrilous claim that John had idled in bed with her while Normandy was being lost. The king had several bastard children, such as Geoffrey, who led troops to Poitou in 1205, but they were all too old to have been fathered during his second marriage, and possibly even during his first. Gifts to women who might have been his mistresses do figure in royal financial accounts, but not until later in his reign. Despite what appears to have been an unusual ménage at Winchester, if we base our conclusions on evidence rather than hearsay, we have to entertain the alarming possibility that, during the early years of his marriage, John may have been both faithful and chaste.[23]

If the latter was ever the case, however, it was no longer so by 1207, for that year the queen became pregnant. She must have conceived at the start of the year, during the festivities at Winchester that had followed the king's jubilant return from France. At some point after March the older Isabella left Winchester for alternative lodgings at Sherborne, and as the time of the queen's confinement approached, John's visits to Winchester became more frequent. In July and August he interrupted his ceaseless round of hunting to pay four visits, and he was back there by the end of September, in time for the birth of the child that arrived on 1 October. To what must have been general rejoicing, it was a boy, christened Henry after his paternal grand-father. At last, at the age of forty, John had a legitimate heir. His dynasty was meant to continue. It was a sure sign of God's favour.[24]

Unfortunately John was still very much out of favour with God's principal representative on earth. Innocent III had reacted with surprising calmness when he had heard about the king's violent expulsion of the monks of Canterbury towards the end of August. True, he had immediately ordered the bishop of Rochester to excommunicate Reginald of Cornhill, Fulk de Cantilupe and all others who had carried out the attack on Church property. But when he wrote about John himself, the pope did so more in sorrow than in anger. With God as his witness, he explained that he really loved John, his 'very dear son in Christ', with the most sincere affection. Indeed, the affection he had shown to the king in the past was such that it had damaged papal relations with other princes (an allusion to Philip Augustus). And yet, despite this consistent love and kindness, John was ungrateful, and had followed foolish advice.

These remarks, written on 27 August, were addressed not to the king himself, but to the bishops of London, Worcester and Ely, a trio seemingly selected because they had acted as papal agents in the past and did not owe their advancement to John. They were instructed to visit the king and remonstrate with him, urging him to accept Stephen Langton as archbishop and to readmit the monks of Canterbury. If he refused to do so, they were to impose an interdict, which meant that there would be no church services. The English clergy would effectively go on strike.[25]

The three bishops cannot have received these instructions until the autumn, and probably did not approach John until 19 October, when all three can be placed in his company by their appearance as witnesses to a royal charter. The king, who had been in Westminster the previous week, was back in Winchester by this date, perhaps dandling his three-week-old son. According to the

Waverley annalist, the bishops approached him tearfully and on bended knee. According to Wendover, John reacted furiously, threatening to confiscate all the clergy's estates, and adding for good measure that he would send any Roman clergy in his realm back to their master with their noses slit and their eyes put out.[26]

Although Wendover has almost certainly sensationalized his account, there is no doubt that the king refused the bishops' request. It is also equally clear that, despite his refusal, the bishops chose not to impose the interdict. This may have been because they feared the consequences. Alternatively, it may have been because they, more so than Innocent, were better able to gauge the mood in England. By the autumn of 1207 John can hardly have been a popular ruler. His government was becoming ever more oppressive. The Forest eyre, as we have seen, had squeezed a great deal of money out of people of all ranks. The general tax known as the Thirteenth had squeezed a great deal more. By the time its yield had been checked at the end of September, it had brought in over £60,000.

Harvesting money on this scale was obviously unpopular. In Lincolnshire men had attempted to evade the tax by depositing their wealth in religious houses. In Warwickshire the evasion was such that the assessment had to be repeated in late May. Some men had refused to pay outright and suffered the harsh penalties threatened at the start of the year. The Exchequer rolls show several individuals imprisoned and others fined. Ruald fitz Alan was deprived of Richmond Castle for refusing to swear to the value of his goods and fined 200 marks. The abbot of Selby was fined forty marks and two palfreys for non-payment, and the monks of Furness lost two of their manors and some of their goods. As these examples imply, much of the resistance to the tax seems to have arisen in the north.[27]

And yet, when it came to choosing between the king and the pope, it seems that most people were on the side of the king. The annalist at Margam Abbey in south Wales, a source deeply hostile to John, nevertheless reports that, on this matter, all the laity favoured the king, and almost all the clergy. Whether because

John's propaganda was more effective, or because of historical precedent, it was clearly felt that the king ought to have a say – the final say, even – in who was archbishop of Canterbury. The archbishop was, after all, not simply a clergyman but a political figure of the foremost importance, whose estates put him on a par with the greatest magnates in the country.[28]

The fact that the Church held vast estates was an added incentive for a cash-hungry king to prolong the dispute. John had already deprived the archbishop of York of his lands in 1207 and driven him into exile before he did the same to the monks of Canterbury. He was also holding the estates of the bishop of Chichester, who had died in August, and those of the bishops of Exeter and Lincoln, both of whom had died the previous year, no doubt keeping their positions vacant as a way of demonstrating his mastery over the appointment process.[29] The bishops of London, Worcester and Ely, knowing the king far better than the pope did, must have realized that his threat to seize the lands of every clergyman in the country was unlikely to be an idle one. After their unsuccessful interview with John in October, they temporized by asking Innocent to clarify the nature of the interdict they were to impose. Did it apply to all religious communities? Did it apply to Wales?

The pope, responding on 19 November, indicated that he was starting to lose patience. He issued a short clarification of the terms of the interdict – yes, it applied to everyone, even the Welsh – and forbade any further delay. With it he dispatched a separate letter to the English bishops, chiding them for their inactivity ('It has come to our hearing that some of you have been tepid and remiss in the matter of the archbishop of Canterbury'), ordering them to put aside fear and to prepare themselves for persecution. He also attempted to open up a new front by addressing another letter to the nobles of England, telling them, 'You should regulate your loyalty to your earthly king so as never to offend your heavenly king.' In view of John's opposition to God, they should not give him their support. John's mind was sick, explained Innocent, and the pope was his doctor.

The king would one day be grateful to them all for administering his medicine, however bitter it seemed on the way down.[30]

Innocent's letters must have reached England shortly after Christmas 1207 or early in the new year of 1208. John had spent the days before Christmas inspecting his new castle at Odiham and celebrated the feast itself at nearby Windsor. It seems unlikely that any of the lay magnates he mixed with during the festive period would have remonstrated with him over his behaviour, but presumably at some point after receiving the pope's stern mandate the bishops of London, Worcester and Ely must have repeated their efforts to persuade the king to change his mind.[31]

To their surprise, perhaps, John now seemed inclined to do so. On 21 January he sent the three bishops a letter, indicating that he was willing to obey Innocent on the matter of Canterbury. Simultaneously, as a conciliatory gesture, he removed Reginald of Cornhill and Fulk de Cantilupe as custodians of the Canterbury lands and replaced them with less offensive agents. There was, however, a proviso. In return for John's compliance, the pope would have to undertake to preserve the king's 'rights, dignity and liberties'. In other words, John seems to have indicated that he would accept Stephen Langton, provided that he was given a cast-iron guarantee of his right to approve all future episcopal elections. His letter was witnessed by seven earls and three other leading barons, a clear display of magnate solidarity in riposte to Innocent's attempt to set the baronage against the king.[32]

Whether or not they passed this message on to the pope, the bishops were sufficiently encouraged to delay until they were joined in March by a papal emissary in the shape of Master Simon Langton, younger brother of the controversial archbishop. Master Simon, as his title suggests, was also a clerk and a scholar, and understood precisely what was at stake. When he appeared before the king at Winchester on 12 March, he made it clear that, when it came to the Canterbury election, there was no room for manoeuvre. 'When we spoke to him about safeguarding our dignity in this matter,' wrote John, 'he said he would not do anything about it unless we placed ourselves entirely at his mercy.' This was in a letter to the men of Kent, issued two days later, explaining why the negotiations had failed, and telling them to listen to Reginald of Cornhill's account of the meeting. The excommunicate sheriff was once again placed in charge of the Canterbury estates. The attempt to conciliate was over.[33]

On Sunday 23 March, in every church in England, the interdict was proclaimed. Henceforth there were to be no church services. Mass would not be performed. Marriages would not be celebrated in church. Confession would not be heard, except in the case of the dying. The dead could not be buried in consecrated ground. Church bells were rung for the last time that Sunday, and were not to be sounded again until the king surrendered.[34]

John had known this was coming and had made sure his retaliation was ready. The following morning, as the interdict began, his agents moved in to seize the goods and lands of every clergyman in the kingdom. In every parish four men were appointed to lock up and guard the Church's barns. At the same moment, the king appears to have let it be known that it was effectively open season on the clergy. 'Religious men and other ordained persons of any kind,' said Roger of Wendover, 'when found travelling on the road, were dragged from their horses, robbed and basely ill-treated by the king's followers, and no one would do them justice.' This sounds like typically sensational stuff from Wendover, but its essential truth is confirmed by a writ issued by John three weeks later, forbidding laymen from abusing clerics, on pain of being hanged from the nearest oak. That the king felt obliged to issue such strong counter-measures suggests that in the short term the clergy must have suffered many assaults at the hands of their lay neighbours.[35]

In the long term it was obviously impossible for the king to occupy and manage the lands of every churchman. After a short while many were able to strike a deal whereby they received their lands back in return for a fine — but only as custodians, allowed to take an agreed portion of the revenues for their sustenance and paying all the profits to the king. John also found a mischievous way to make even more money out of the clergy by seizing all their mistresses and girlfriends and holding them to ransom. Since clerics were supposed to be celibate there could be no official objection to this underhand move. Moralists had to reserve their criticism for those churchmen who rushed to pay for the release of their lovers.[36]

There is no sign that the laity were in any way bothered by the interdict or by the king's reprisals against the clergy. Some lay magnates, indeed, were given custody of confiscated Church land, and probably allowed to keep the profits for themselves.[37] Nevertheless, John may well have been troubled by Innocent's attempt to turn his nobility against him. At a time when men were already expressing their dissatisfaction about the general oppressiveness of his government, the idea that the pope might absolve them of their loyalty altogether must have been a disturbing one. According to Roger of Wendover, once the interdict had been imposed, the king was sufficiently worried that he sent out agents to those magnates of whom he was suspicious and demanded hostages from them in the form of their sons or nephews. At length they came to the home of a nobleman called William de Briouze and made this demand, but before he could answer, his wife, Matilda, responded on his behalf. 'I will not deliver up my sons to your lord, King John,' she told the royal messengers, 'because he basely murdered his nephew, Arthur, whom he ought to have taken care of honourably.'[38]

8

A Deed of Shame

1202–1203

The news that John had captured Arthur, the Lusignans and hundreds of their supporters spread rapidly from Mirebeau in all directions, bringing joy to the king's adherents and despair to his enemies. In Normandy those barons who had remained behind to resist the invasion of Philip Augustus were elated when the message arrived, and immediately sent it on to the French camp at Arques, where (as intended) it had the opposite effect. Ralph de Lusignan, hearing of the misfortune that had befallen his kinsmen, reportedly fell silent and had to have a lie-down in his tent. Philip became immensely angry, realizing that Arthur's capture meant his own campaign must come to an end. At once he called off his assault on the castle at Arques, and in his fury ordered his siege engines be smashed to pieces.[1]

John meanwhile was already heading northwards towards Normandy, taking with him his horde of high-status captives. By 10 August 1202, nine days after Mirebeau, he was at Falaise, and the mighty stone donjon built by his ancestor Henry I, which now became Arthur's prison. That same day he sent Hugh de Lusignan to Caen, another of Henry's great towers, ordering its constable to clear out any other prisoners being held there, and giving strict instructions to admit no one without the approval of his trusted henchman, Hugh de Neville. Dozens of less important prisoners were distributed in other castles throughout the duchy, and dozens more were sent across the Channel to be kept in castles all over England: Bristol, Wallingford, Corfe, Nottingham, Colchester, Pickering, Sherborne, Southampton, Marlborough, Portchester, Norwich, Carlisle, Peveril, Bamburgh, Oxford, Northampton, Windsor and Devizes. John had captured so many of his enemies that there were scarcely enough strongholds to contain them.[2]

Even before the king had reached Falaise, however, concerns were being raised about the way these prisoners were being treated. Roger of Wendover reports that when they left Mirebeau they were not only shackled and chained, but placed in carts, 'a new and unusual way of travelling'. Security was of course essential, but John, in the flush of his triumph, seems to have set out deliberately to humiliate his enemies, parading them through every town and village. 'When the king arrived at Chinon,' says *The History of William Marshal*, 'he kept his prisoners in such a horrible manner and in such abject confinement that it seemed an indignity and a disgrace to all those with him who witnessed his cruelty.'[3]

One person in particular who was concerned about this treatment was William des Roches. William, it will be recalled, was the man who had brokered a peace between John and Arthur in the autumn of 1199, negotiating secretly with the king and successfully bringing in his nephew. That peace had proved extremely short-lived, because Arthur had fled on hearing that his uncle intended to keep him in prison.[4] William, however, had stayed in the king's camp and kept his position as seneschal of Anjou. He was, in the opinion of contemporaries, a fine knight. He was also, according to more than one source, the true author of the victory at Mirebeau, advising John on how to mount the attack and fighting valiantly when it was carried out, on the understanding that the king would be similarly guided by his advice when it came to exploiting the final outcome. With this understanding in mind he had approached John afterwards to discuss the fate of the prisoners. According to *The History of William Marshal*, he began by reminding the king of the events of 1199, when he had delivered Arthur on condition that they should all be friends.[5]

John responded, not unreasonably, that a lot had happened since 1199, saying 'my nephew has done me much wrong'. But William persisted. In opposing his uncle, he suggested, Arthur had been the tool of others and had not been acting on his own account. If the king would let him take care of it, William was sure he could bring everything to a satisfactory conclusion. John, says the *History*, agreed to this, but then kept putting the matter off. William was asked to wait until they reached Chinon; at Chinon he was told to wait until Le Mans. By the time they arrived at Falaise, at which point Arthur was imprisoned in the castle, shackled with three sets of manacles, William must have concluded that he was being played for a fool, and that the king had no intention of heeding his advice or handing over his nephew. A few days later he left John's court and returned to his own estates.[6]

The king soon realized that des Roches had departed and appointed others to take over his role as governor of Anjou.[7] Given their reported exchanges, John may have anticipated this development and reckoned that it was a price worth paying to keep Arthur securely under lock and key. As far as the king was concerned, the only mistake he had made in 1199 was leaving his nephew unguarded. Clearly there was no way he was going to take that chance a second time.

In any case, John seemed to be on an unstoppable roll. Immediately after Mirebeau he had dispatched some of his troops on a punitive raid into Brittany, where they had ravaged the countryside and reduced several towns to ashes; by the time of William des Roches' desertion, the leading barons of Brittany were seeking safe conduct to come and negotiate. Meanwhile the king, having delivered his prisoners to Normandy, had returned south with similar hostile intent. In mid-August he burned down Le Mans as punishment for having earlier received his enemies. A few days later he pushed further south to Tours. Philip Augustus had installed a garrison there after his retreat from Normandy, and for a short time there was a violent struggle between these men and John's forces, until eventually the latter triumphed. Again the city was put to the torch. At the start of September the king struck west along the Loire until he came to Angers, which was similarly assaulted and occupied. Around the same time he received news from Poitou that one of his few remaining enemies, the viscount of Limoges, had been captured. On every front his military successes were multiplying.[8]

Satisfied that his affairs in Anjou were prospering, in late September John returned to Normandy. His precise reasons for doing so are obscure, but his appearance at Verneuil suggests that he was attending to the defences on the duchy's eastern frontier. Philip Augustus had taken many castles there in the course of his invasion during the summer, and although the French king had now withdrawn, there was as yet no talk of truce or peace.[9]

Towards the end of October, John discovered why. William des Roches and the nobles of Brittany, both angry over the continued detention of Arthur, had made common cause and were attacking the king's towns and castles. They were joined by lots of other nobles in Anjou, Maine and Touraine, who had been equally incensed by his destruction of their principal cities during the summer. John left Normandy and hastened south again,[10] but by the time he reached the Loire it was too late: des Roches and the Bretons had occupied Angers and the count of Amboise had taken Tours. Worse still for the king, he seems to have been unable to do anything to reverse these losses. For the first half of November he sat at Saumur and for the second half at Chinon. In the middle of the month he received the news that his favourite mercenary captain had been captured.[11]

It may have been at this juncture that John ordered the mutilation of Arthur. According to Ralph of Coggeshall, the king's advisers, seeing the scale of the disturbances that the Bretons were causing, and realizing that no reliable peace could be made with them, recommended that he give the order for Arthur to be blinded and castrated, their notion being that this would render the young duke unable to govern, and thus induce his supporters to submit. The story is well known because it was later taken up by the Tudor chronicler Holinshed, and from there by Shakespeare, who made it the dramatic hinge of his play *King John*. Coggeshall is, however, the only contemporary source, and so needs to be regarded with some caution. He continues his account by explaining that John, provoked by the ceaseless attacks of his enemies into a furious rage, gave the hateful order, and sent three of his servants to Falaise to carry it out. Two of them fled rather than have to do so, but the third eventually came to the castle, which was being kept by the king's chamberlain, Hubert de Burgh. When Hubert and his knights learned the nature of the newcomer's business they were moved to pity for Arthur, who in turn became aware of what was intended. At first he broke down in tears, but then leapt up and grappled with the man who had been sent to maim him. The knights managed to pull them apart, and Hubert ordered that the unwelcome visitor be ejected.

Hubert, says Coggeshall, then made a bold decision. Realizing that the order, if carried out, would cause terrible damage to John's reputation, he decided that Arthur would remain unharmed. The king, he was convinced, must have spoken in anger and would soon come to regret it. In the meantime, however, wishing to quell the rebellion of the Bretons, he pretended that the order had been obeyed, and let it be known that Arthur had died as a result of his injuries. Trumpets were blown in every castle and town to mark his passing, his clothes were donated to the local leper house, and it was announced that his body had been taken to the nearby abbey of St André for burial.

But – unsurprisingly – the news that Arthur had been killed failed to calm the Bretons, who raged with even greater fury than before, 'swearing that they would never stop fighting the king of England, who had dared to commit such a horrible crime against their lord, his own nephew'. And so, explains Coggeshall, after a fortnight or so, it was decided to proclaim that Arthur was in fact still alive and unharmed.[12]

Such is Coggeshall's story. If there is nothing in the way of contemporary evidence to corroborate it, nor is there anything to contradict it. Certain points of detail, such as the mention of the abbey of St André, suggest it was unlikely to simply have been invented by a chronicler in Essex. The original source, it has been suggested, may well have been Hubert de Burgh himself, since he is the person who emerges in the most positive light.[13]

Is the story, in general terms, credible? On the one hand, many people in the Middle Ages suffered such acts of mutilation. In England, as we've seen, you could lose your eyes and genitals for taking a deer in the royal Forest. Such punishments, however, were almost never applied to people of high status. Since the early eleventh century in France, and since the Norman Conquest in England, it had been morally and politically unacceptable for one nobleman to kill another who was at his mercy. Knights might die in battle, but usually their armour protected them until the fighting was over, and at that point the victors would take their defeated opponents prisoner. Sometimes they would release them in return for a ransom; other times they might detain them indefinitely. What they would not do was kill or maim them. Even kings with ferocious reputations respected this taboo. William the Conqueror, responsible for the deaths of countless thousands of ordinary Englishmen, ordered the execution of only one English earl, and suffered some opprobrium as a result. His son, Henry I, was scarcely less brutal. As well as ordering the mass castration of his moneyers, he is said to have disposed of a burgess of Rouen by throwing him off the top of a castle tower. Yet when Henry captured his elder brother and rival, Robert Curthose, he had no option other than to keep him captive, and Robert remained incarcerated until his death almost thirty years later.[14]

Detaining prisoners indefinitely was not a problem, provided you held the whip hand. A powerful ruler could be confident that a subject who surrendered a hostage would remain obedient simply in the hope of one day obtaining the hostage's release. John's difficulty in 1202 was that, in spite of his triumph at Mirebeau, his enemies were still very powerful. When the Bretons realized, as William des Roches had done, that John had no intention of releasing Arthur, they simply resumed their war against him. John had foreseen this possibility during the brief period of negotiations in August, when he had warned the Bretons 'not to do anything whereby evil may befall us or our nephew, Arthur'. His enemies had decided to take the risk that he was bluffing. It is not difficult to imagine how the king, enraged at their invasion of Anjou, yet powerless to contest it, might have decided to prove them wrong.[15]

The renewed rebellion of the Bretons may therefore have prompted John into ordering Arthur's mutilation, which may in turn have prompted Hubert de Burgh to announce that the duke was dead. If something of this kind did happen, however, it is clear, as Coggeshall says, that it failed to bring the Bretons to heel. In early December the king withdrew to Normandy, leaving Tours and Angers in the hands of his enemies.[16]

What is certain is that the renewed rebellion of the Bretons prompted John to take a gamble in completely the opposite direction. Much like the followers of Arthur, the followers of Hugh and Geoffrey de Lusignan had been seeking to intercede on behalf of their imprisoned masters since August. At that time, with his affairs going well, John had probably been disinclined to listen to them, but by the autumn his deteriorating fortunes had led him to negotiate in earnest. On 6 November he had given orders for Hugh de Lusignan to be released from his strict custody at Caen and brought to him at Saumur, heavily guarded, for talks with his brother, Ralph. Conditions of release must have been discussed, and by 23 December – at which point the king was in Caen to celebrate Christmas – castles had been surrendered to him and he was ready to receive their men as hostages. By the middle of January, the hostages must have been delivered, for at that point both Hugh and Geoffrey de Lusignan were freed.[17]

As the precautions imply, this was clearly a very risky move. John and the Lusignans had been bitter enemies ever since his decision to steal Hugh's fiancée and marry her himself. But since the capture of Arthur at Mirebeau, and because of his determination never to release him, John had made new enemies among the barons of Anjou, particularly William des Roches. He could not afford to be at war with so many men at once. The detention of Arthur, which ought to have ended the threat of his succession once and for all, was clearly paramount. It therefore followed that, in order to maintain a hard line with Arthur's supporters, the king would have to show leniency to the Lusignans. By granting them their freedom, and holding out the prospect that their recently surrendered castles and hostages might one day be restored, he hoped to be able to guarantee their faithful service. Once they were back in Poitou, they could attack his enemies in Anjou from the south, while he simultaneously advanced from Normandy in the north, and between them they would crush those who still entertained the hope that Arthur might one day be freed. The king's writs show that he was planning to advance from Argentan, close to Normandy's southern border, at the start of February.[18]

But before this happened, his plans suffered a massive setback. In mid-January John was in the vicinity of Argentan when he heard that his queen was in danger. Isabella was apparently at Chinon, in the midst of the king's enemies, much as his mother had been at Mirebeau six months earlier.[19] As on that occasion John set out immediately with a large army of knights and mercenaries, hoping to avert a disastrous capture. He had not even travelled as far as Le Mans, however, when the next hammer blow fell. Count Robert of Alençon, a Norman nobleman with whom he had dined earlier that same day, had defected. The town of Alençon, which the king had left just a few miles to his rear, had been occupied by French forces.

'Alas! Alack!' cried John, according to *The History of William Marshal*. 'What a cruel act of treachery! Robert has greatly wronged me!' The chronicler's account of his anger is borne out by the official record: months later, the king was dating his charters with the phrase 'the year when Count Robert betrayed us'. With a French garrison now cutting off his retreat, John was suddenly afraid to go further forward, fearing that his enemies would attack him on the road to Chinon. As it was, the situation was partially retrieved by the heroism of one of his knights, Peter de Préaux, who managed to reach Isabella at Chinon and deliver her safely to Le Mans. From there the king and his army managed to return to Normandy, avoiding Alençon by taking a circuitous route.[20]

The revolt of the count of Alençon was not quite the total disaster it could have been, in that neither Isabella nor John himself was captured. It did, however, spell the end for the king's plan of a combined offensive with the Lusignans against his enemies in Anjou. Alençon lies on the Norman frontier, controlling the main route south, and Count Robert had probably been expected to play a leading role in the campaign, to judge from *The History of William Marshal*'s comment that he had been given money by the king just days before his defection.[21]

With his military options shrinking fast, John made for Falaise, where Arthur was still being held. According to Roger of Wendover, the occasion for this visit was another volte-face in strategy. The king, says the chronicler, ordered his nephew to be brought into his presence and spoke to him kindly, promising him many honours if he would abandon Philip Augustus and recognize John, his uncle, as his lord. In other words, late in the day, Arthur was being offered the sort of deal advocated by William des Roches the previous summer – leniency in return for loyalty – evidently in the hope that, if he accepted, it would persuade des Roches, the Bretons and their increasing numerous followers to stand down.

But it was too late. Arthur, says Wendover, replied to his uncle's offer with indignation and threats. (Perhaps not surprising, if Coggeshall's story of the earlier attempt to mutilate him is true.) Whatever honours John had proposed were not enough; he, Arthur, was the rightful heir to the whole Angevin Empire, and unless his uncle resigned it all to him, he would never enjoy a moment's peace. At these words, the chronicler continues, the king was very troubled, and commanded that his nephew should be taken to Rouen and confined in the castle there. John's writs confirm that he did indeed make directly for Rouen at this point.[22]

They also attest to the terrible nature of his anger. On 30 January, the day after his arrival at Falaise, and presumably after his reported exchanges with Arthur, the king sent letters to Hugh de Neville, who until recently had been guarding Hugh de Lusignan at Caen. Neville was ordered to cross the Channel to England, taking with him two other prisoners from Mirebeau, Warin de Craon and Maurice de Basuen, who were to be deposited in Corfe Castle. Five days later, after he had reached Rouen, John dispatched a barrage of writs to England, directed to the constables of eighteen castles, requiring them to send a further twenty-two named individuals to the same place, ignoring all previous orders about their custody. Finally, he wrote to the constable of Corfe 'that he should do what Thomas, clerk of our Chamber, and Hugh de Neville will tell him on the king's behalf concerning the prisoners that have been delivered to him'. The content of these orders, which could not be committed to writing, is revealed in a single line in the annals of Margam Abbey in south Wales: 'twenty-two of the noblest and strongest in arms were starved to death in Corfe Castle, so that not one of them escaped'.[23]

To kill men by starvation was clearly a cruel and unusual punishment; records of similar incidents are rare. According to Ralph of Coggeshall, Richard I had condemned one of the men who had supported John's rebellion against him to such a fate, after the man in question had tried to frustrate Richard's release from prison, and professed his unshakeable devotion to John's cause.[24] John's action in 1203 was clearly on a far greater scale, and seemingly provoked by the defiant rejection of his overtures to Arthur. The men John sent to Corfe, to judge from their surnames, were from Brittany and Anjou, so the king's intention, if it had any political dimension at all, was presumably to demonstrate to Arthur's supporters in those provinces the dreadful price of their continued disloyalty.

Loyalty to John was becoming an increasingly scarce commodity. Even within Normandy, disaffection was starting to spread. Few men, it is true, had followed the count of Alençon into revolt, and he in any case was a frontier lord whose family ties linked him to Arthur's supporters in Maine and Anjou.[25] But, at the same time, few men were rallying to their duke to help him defend his remaining territories. There were, no doubt, long-term reasons for this reluctance. No one in Normandy could have forgotten John's attempt to usurp Richard's place ten years earlier, and how he had refused to help defend the duchy against Philip Augustus. But there were also more immediate reasons for the king's unpopularity. As his vassals and allies in other regions had deserted him, John had become increasingly reliant on merce-naries, even to the extent of appointing such men to positions of public authority. On 4 December 1202, the day he had departed from Chinon and abandoned Anjou for Normandy, he had appointed one of his most notorious mercenary captains, Martin Algais, as seneschal of Gascony. Another mercenary captain of equal notoriety named Louvrecaire accompanied the king north, and was given safe conduct to bring his plunder into Normandy. When John withdrew to Rouen at the start of February, Louvrecaire and his routiers remained in Falaise, from where they proceeded to terrorize the interior of the duchy, living off the land like an army of occupation. Twenty-five years later, a letter written by a burgess of Caen recalled how these men 'violated the wives of knights and laymen, and carried off their goods … if they came across a man, they stole his horse or seized his plough, and said he should look to the king for compensation'. The peaceful, well-governed heartlands of Normandy, previously untouched by war, had been given over to freebooters.[26]

For all of February and most of March, John remained in Rouen or its immediate neighbourhood. Despised by his own subjects, he distrusted them in turn, and became increasingly reluctant to travel even within Normandy. On the few occasions when he did venture out of the capital, he went accompanied by a mercenary band, and moved along minor roads taking roundabout routes, always suspecting that around the next bend an ambush might be waiting. 'A man who does not know whom he has to fear', commented *The History of William Marshal*, 'is bound to fear everybody.'[27]

Every day, says the *History*, the king saw his duchy getting worse as the result of war, and the list of defections grew. By the middle of February, he had heard the worst from Poitou: the Lusignans, despite their promises, their hostages and their surrendered castles, were once again in rebellion. In March, leading rebels from Poitou, Maine, Anjou and Brittany travelled to Paris to swear allegiance to Philip Augustus, who was evidently preparing the ground for a major assault. Among the list of names we find both Geoffrey de Lusignan and William des Roches, who had fought on opposite sides at Mirebeau just eight months earlier. It is a remarkable testament to John's political ineptitude that he had driven these former enemies to unite against him in such a short space of time.[28]

It was during these dark and desperate days that Arthur was finally killed. The manner in which he met his end is shrouded in mystery, for few chroniclers knew anything in the way of details. Roger of Wendover and Matthew Paris, for instance, who would surely have relished telling a story that blackened John's reputation, could report very little. Wendover says simply that Arthur disappeared after he was taken to Rouen. He adds, however, that later a rumour ran around all of France that John had killed him with his own hand. That was indeed the story told by the French chronicler William the Breton, who relates how the king had taken his nephew out alone one night in a boat on the Seine, run him through with a sword and thrown the body into the river.[29]

The one other place that this story occurs is in the chronicle kept at Margam Abbey. According to its anonymous author, John killed his nephew 'after dinner on the Thursday before Easter, when he was drunk and possessed by the Devil'. Afterwards he tied a heavy stone to the body and dumped it into the Seine, where it was later found by a fisherman, and taken secretly for burial in a nearby priory.[30]

The existence of two similar stories, in which the king personally kills Arthur and dumps his body into the river, recorded by writers living so far apart, might lead us to assume that they were independent, and that therefore their content is broadly true. In fact, the two stories almost certainly originate from a single source: William de Briouze.

William de Briouze was one of John's greatest subjects, a magnate whose pedigree stretched back as far as the Norman Conquest and beyond. His ancestral estates were at Briouze in Normandy, but the bulk of his fortune lay in England and Wales. His lands in Wales explain why he features so prominently in the annals of Margam, for the abbey lay within his lordship. Towards the end of his life Briouze ended up in France at the court of Philip Augustus, thus explaining how he came to the attention of William the Breton.[31]

Briouze had been a close associate of Richard I, but he became even closer to John. Present at the time of Richard's death at Châlus in 1199, he was, according to the Margam annals, the key figure in persuading the rest of the old king's followers to support John as his successor. John was certainly very generous to Briouze at the start of his reign, rewarding him richly with lands in England, Wales and Ireland, and Briouze in consequence stuck close to his new master: down to 1203 no layman witnessed more royal charters. Briouze had been with John at Mirebeau and had been personally responsible for capturing Arthur. He was still in the king's company the following Easter, when Arthur is said to have died. In short, if anyone was well placed to know the truth about what happened to Arthur, it was William de Briouze.[32]

Whether or not he told the truth is another matter. The striking thing about William the Breton's account is the extent to which it exonerates Briouze and makes him a voice of concern for Arthur's welfare. In this version of the story, once they had arrived in Rouen, Briouze declares that he will be responsible for Arthur no longer, hands him over to John safe and sound, and then retires to his own estates. But this last part, at least, is demonstrably not true. From his witnessing of royal documents we can see that Briouze was present in Rouen the whole time.[33]

Since Briouze was clearly lying about his absence, there is no good reason to believe his claim that the king personally did away with his nephew when no one else was looking. It is more likely that the decision to kill Arthur was taken by John in consultation with his closest advisers, just as we are told had been the case when the earlier order had been given to mutilate him. One of those advisers was evidently William de Briouze. Other men who were with the king at this moment, revealed in the administrative sources, included his half-brother William Longsword, and Reginald of Cornhill, later to become the scourge of the monks of Canterbury. One person in particular who stands out from the list of names is Geoffrey fitz Peter, the justiciar of England, who suddenly appears in John's presence just before the time of Arthur's murder and then disappears soon afterwards. Geoffrey's duties as justiciar (in effect, the king's regent) ordinarily detained him in England; only on one previous occasion had he crossed the Channel to consult with John. His fleeting appearance in Rouen at Easter 1203 suggests he had been summoned there to approve some especially important piece of business.[34]

If the decision to end Arthur's life was taken in committee, who actually killed him, if not King John? A century later, when everybody involved was long dead, a Yorkshire chronicler called Walter of Guisborough named the murderer as Peter de Maulay. This testimony has been previously dismissed as too late to be trustworthy, but Maulay, who lived until 1241, later became a leading baron in Yorkshire, and his principal castle at Mulgrave lay not far from Guisborough Priory. He was certainly in John's employ by the spring of 1203, and rose rapidly in the king's service thereafter. In the absence of any other evidence, he would seem to be the likeliest culprit.[35]

Who killed Arthur cannot be said with absolute certainty. That he was dead by the middle of April 1203 is amply clear. On 16 April John sent a messenger to several of his leading supporters: Hubert de Burgh, now serving as constable of Chinon; Martin Algais, the mercenary seneschal of Gascony; the seneschals of

Anjou and Poitou; the archbishop of Bordeaux; and even his elderly mother, Eleanor of Aquitaine. All these people were instructed to give credence to what the messenger, John de Valerant, would tell them about the king's affairs, which were suddenly prospering. 'By the grace of God,' says the king, 'things are going better for us than he can tell you.' The letter was witnessed by William de Briouze.[36]

In fact, as all of his southern officials could have told him, it was already the beginning of the end. Even as these letters were being drafted, Philip Augustus and his allies were invading Anjou. In mid-April the French king sailed along the Loire and seized the castle at Saumur. William des Roches and the Bretons were already advancing from the west; by the end of the month they had taken Le Mans. John's rickety administration in the region collapsed completely, cutting him off from his officials further south.[37] Philip immediately swung his army north to begin seizing castles in eastern Normandy, finding in several cases that their disillusioned keepers were ready to surrender them without a fight. By the end of the summer he was drawing up his siege engines outside the walls of Château Gaillard.

To a large extent, therefore, the death of Arthur made no difference to the loss of the Angevin Empire. It was not known about in France or Brittany when the French king and his allies unleashed what was to be their final assault in the spring of 1203, and so cannot have been a trigger for war. Of course, once that war was under way, and rumours of Arthur's murder began to circulate, they no doubt added to the resolve of John's enemies. By the autumn of 1203 Philip clearly suspected that the disturbing stories he was hearing might be true: in a charter issued that October he referred to Arthur 'if he still lives'. By the spring of 1204, once Château Gaillard had fallen, he was convinced that they were fact. When John's envoys approached him in April in a desperate attempt to forestall his advance, he told them they could have peace only if Arthur was handed over to him alive. 'He was absolutely furious about Arthur's death', says Ralph of Coggeshall, and there is even some evidence to suggest the French king may have passed sentence against John *in absentia* in his court. But this was simply to add justification to a process that was inevitable and almost complete. A few weeks later and Normandy was conquered.[38]

If Arthur's fate ultimately made little difference to the loss of the empire, it nevertheless made a crucial difference to King John. In doing away with his nephew, John had broken one of society's fundamental taboos, with dire consequences for his reputation. The decision may have been taken in committee, behind closed doors, and the deed itself done in secret. But inevitably, once Arthur had disappeared, the rumours about him began to spread, and information leaked out. In the end, everyone must have heard what had happened to him, but if they were wise they did not speak of it. Those who were obliged to hand over hostages to the king after 1203 must have done so with trepidation, knowing what extremes he was capable of. That was apparently why, five years later, the wife of William de Briouze refused to surrender her sons to his agents. Her mistake was to say publicly what had hitherto only been whispered in private.

9

The Enemy Within?

1208—1210

William de Briouze was acutely aware of the potentially disastrous consequences of his wife's incautious words. 'You have spoken like a foolish woman against our lord the king', he told her, before assuring the royal messengers that he was prepared to make amends to John for whatever offence he had caused. Such at least is the story told by Roger of Wendover. The messengers, continues the chronicler, returned to the king and told him all they had heard, at which John was predictably enraged, and sent knights to seize William and his family.[1]

As we shall see, there are good reasons for supposing that the essence of Wendover's story may be true. The king did indeed demand hostages from William de Briouze in the spring of 1208 and also sent agents in pursuit of his family. Moreover he persecuted William's wife, Matilda, with a malevolence which was exceptional even by his highly competitive standards. Where Wendover erred was in assuming that the demand for hostages was the cause of the rift between the two men. In fact their quarrel had begun several months earlier, and its roots lay in Ireland.

Ireland had been left in a state of limbo ever since the death of John's older brother Geoffrey. It was Geoffrey's death in the summer of 1186, rather than the failure of John's expedition to

Ireland the previous year, that had finally put paid to Henry II's plan for his youngest son to rule there as a king in his own right. Thereafter John became simply 'lord of Ireland', a less august title which always took second place to 'count of Mortain' in his charters. While Henry lived, John exercised no meaningful authority at all there, his acts always subject to review. After his father's death he enjoyed considerably greater power, rewarding several of his followers with Irish lordships, until his wings were again clipped in 1194 with the return of an angry Richard. By the time of his accession in 1199, Ireland had become the Wild West of the British Isles — an unruly frontier where men with the right talents could carve out new lordships at sword-point, chiefly at the expense of the natives, but also on occasion at the expense of each other.[2]

During the early years of his reign, when he was preoccupied with securing and defending his inheritance on the Continent, John had little time to think about Ireland. He relied on favourite magnates to uphold his interests there, granting them extensive territories to govern more or less as they pleased, though often setting them against one another to prevent any of them becoming too powerful. Grants of land at the expense of the Irish were a useful way to reward those men who were serving him in France.[3] Thus it was at the start of 1201 that he made such a grant to William de Briouze, giving him the former Irish kingdom of Limerick.[4]

Once his continental lands were lost, however, John began paying greater attention to the remaining parts of his empire, looking to see how they might contribute to his depleted coffers, and if they could be better administered. From that point on Ireland came under greater royal scrutiny and stricter management. In the second half of 1204, for example, the king ordered the construction of a new stone castle at Dublin, intending that it should be the future seat of royal government. At the same time he made Dublin the only place in Ireland where coins could be minted, forbidding the earlier practice whereby some magnates had minted their own, and introduced to Ireland the same legal and administrative forms that applied in England.[5]

William de Briouze was among those who immediately felt this change in the direction of royal policy, when on 2 November 1204 John ordered him to return the city of Limerick. This no doubt rankled with Briouze, but in this instance he could raise little objection, for the city had been not been included in the king's original grant, and he was only holding it at John's pleasure. Worse followed in April 1206, when the king ordered his justiciar in Ireland to begin 'shiring' the south-west of the country – that is, introducing the local government structures that had long been in use in England, with a view to increasing the Crown's authority. In establishing the boundary between the lordship of Limerick and the neighbouring lordship of Cork, the king ordered the confiscation of five territories that had previously belonged to Briouze.[6]

The justiciar, Meiler fitz Henry, set about tearing Briouze down to size with a certain relish. Meiler had been one of the first Anglo-Norman settlers in Ireland, and had played a leading role in wresting Limerick from the Irish more than thirty years earlier. A cousin of Gerald of Wales, he no doubt shared the chronicler's opinion that Briouze was a latecomer and an interloper – one of those men who, in Gerald's words, 'owed their position more to luck than ability, and their success to other people's endeavours rather than their own'. In the winter of 1206–7 Meiler launched an assault on Limerick and took the whole lordship by force.[7]

Briouze himself was not in Ireland when this attack was carried out. (As far as can be seen, his only visit to Limerick had been a flying visit to take possession of the lordship in 1201.) At the start of 1207 he was evidently still in England with John, and still very much in favour. On 12 February the king wrote to Meiler fitz Henry, explaining that Briouze ('who has served us well and laudably') had complained to him about the invasion of his lands, and instructing the justiciar to make amends.[8]

But in Ireland the fighting was already spreading in all directions. Briouze may not have been present in Limerick in person but he had powerful friends to defend his interests there. Around the time he had been granted the lordship he had married his daughter, Margaret, to Walter de Lacy. Walter was the eldest son of Hugh de Lacy, the early conquistador whose ambition and success had caused so much anxiety to both Henry II and John down to his death in 1186. Despite John's initial opposition Walter had succeeded to his father's lordship in Meath, as well as other lands in England, Wales and Normandy. After his marriage to Margaret, he and Briouze had come to a reciprocal arrangement, whereby he looked after the Briouze lands in Ireland and his father-in-law did the same for the Lacy estates in England and Wales.[9]

When the justiciar had attacked Limerick in 1207 Walter had upheld his end of the bargain and struck back hard: at one point he and his tenants in Meath had besieged Meiler in one of his own castles. Walter was joined in this struggle by his younger brother, Hugh de Lacy, who as recently as 1205 had been created earl of Ulster after John had fallen out with the previous holder of the title. And by February 1207 the two brothers had been joined by William Marshal. The Marshal was the greatest of all the Anglo-Norman landowners in Ireland, thanks to his marriage in 1189 to Isabella, daughter of Richard fitz Gilbert, the conqueror of Leinster. He too had suffered losses at Meiler's hands and had come to add his weight to the resistance. By the summer of 1207 what had begun as an attempt to increase royal authority had escalated into an all-out war between the justiciar and many of Ireland's major barons.[10]

Once it became clear that the situation in Ireland was spinning out of control, and that it could not be fixed simply by sending a few more crossbowmen across the Irish Sea, John ordered the leading figures on both sides to appear before him in England. Walter de Lacy did so early in the summer and was apparently reconciled; William Marshal and Meiler fitz Henry crossed in the autumn. In November all three men and many other barons from Ireland were present in a council at the royal manor of Woodstock, during which the king laid down the law about the way the country was to be governed in future. He also used the occasion to cut the Marshal down to size, persuading several of the earl's followers to desert him by making them new grants of land.[11]

It seems very likely that William de Briouze was also present at this meeting – he witnessed royal grants on other occasions both before and after that autumn. His relationship with John, however, was hitting the rocks. (The author of *The History of William Marshal* says that Briouze was 'badly embroiled' with the king at this time.) The likely cause was the behaviour of Briouze's seneschal in Limerick, Geoffrey Marsh: on 13 November, as soon as the council had ended, John gave orders for Geoffrey to be arrested, not only for various acts of war, but also for having ignored the summons to appear before him in England. To effect this arrest the king sent Meiler fitz Henry back to Ireland, and at the same time he actively forbade the Marshal and other magnates from leaving his court. His intention was that the justiciar should win the war while his opponents were detained in England.[12]

The Marshal dutifully complied, remaining at court throughout the winter, despite the fact that no one there dared to speak to him because he was out of favour. According to *The History of William Marshal*, John's behaviour during this time was despicable. At one point early in the new year he called the earl over to him and told him with a laugh that he had received news from Ireland: many of the Marshal's men had been killed in a clash with Meiler's forces. This was untrue, and in fact John was not in a position to know anything of the sort, since no ships had been able to cross the Irish Sea during the winter months. The earl, greatly troubled by the king's false report, nevertheless responded with calmness and courtesy, pointing out that the men in question had been the king's faithful subjects.[13]

William de Briouze appears to have coped less well in the face of similar royal provocation. On 5 December John granted part of the lordship of Limerick to Walter de Lacy, a move which was presumably intended to set Briouze and his son-in-law against each other. Briouze was at court until Christmas – he witnessed a royal charter on 26 December – but must have left soon thereafter. According to the well-informed annalist at Worcester Priory, the king suspected that he had ordered Geoffrey Marsh to seize the city of Limerick and other castles in Ireland, and summoned William to answer this charge. Briouze refused, and instead went to his lands in south Wales, where he began to fortify his castles.[14]

By 20 February, with news from Ireland still lacking, John had decided to deal with the situation there himself. On that date he wrote to all the mariners of the Welsh coast, forbidding them from crossing the Irish Sea for anyone else, and instructing them to be ready to transport him and his troops on 16 March. 'If you do otherwise,' his letters concluded, 'we will have your bodies hanged, and those of the owners of your ships, and all your possessions taken for our own use without compensation.'[15]

But before these preparations had been completed, news from Ireland finally arrived. The king's justiciar, Meiler fitz Henry, had been defeated. The men of William Marshal had appealed for help to the earl of Ulster, Hugh de Lacy, who had ridden to their relief. Meiler had been taken prisoner in the fighting and forced to conclude a humiliating peace with the Marshal's wife, Countess Isabella, handing over his son as a hostage.[16]

The defeat of his justiciar forced John into a climbdown. The planned expedition to Ireland was called off, and instead the king sought to come to terms with the magnates he had been detaining and harassing. William Marshal, having behaved with calm restraint throughout the crisis, was quickly received back into royal favour; Walter de Lacy was also rehabilitated, at least in part.[17] A question mark continued to hang over Lacy because of his close connection with William de Briouze, who at this stage was still out in the cold, defiantly holed up in his Welsh castles. Efforts were clearly made to persuade him to come in. On 17 March the sheriff of Gloucester, who had evidently invaded Briouze's lands on royal orders, was told to restore one of the manors he had seized. Two days later Walter de Lacy succeeded in bringing in Briouze's eldest son, also named William, as a hostage. Other friends and relatives were at court at this time, presumably trying to intercede for the older William and arrange terms for his surrender.[18] These efforts clearly failed. By the middle of April the sheriff of Gloucester was once again advancing into Wales, this time in concert with the sheriff of Shropshire, leading what amounted to a sizeable royal army to attack Briouze's lands.[19]

These attacks were enough to persuade the former favourite to submit. On 22 or 23 April, his friends and relatives (this time including his wife, Matilda) again appeared before the king to seek terms. By this point John had arrived in Gloucester, and a few days later, when he was at Hereford, Briouze came in. He agreed to surrender three of his Welsh castles – Hay, Brecon and Radnor – and to pay 1,000 marks to the sheriff of Gloucester to compensate him for the cost of the recent expedition. He also managed to secure the release of his eldest son, but only by handing over six other hostages, including two of his grandsons. It was hardly a heart-warming reconciliation, but it nonetheless meant that the two men were at peace – for the time being.[20]

One thing that makes John's quarrel with William de Briouze especially interesting is that, as well as the usual royal administrative records and chronicle accounts, we also have the king's own version of events. In the autumn of 1210, by which point their relationship had broken down irreparably, John issued an extraordinary public letter, in which he attempted to justify his decision to go against Briouze in the spring of 1208. Unsurprisingly, he chose not to talk about the proxy war in Ireland, nor about Briouze's attempt to start a revolt in the Welsh March. In John's account, the cause of contention was not political but financial. Briouze, the king explained, had owed him a great deal of money. In return for the grant of Limerick in 1201 he had agreed to pay 5,000 marks, and was also answerable for the rent of the city of Limerick. But, alas, despite being granted reasonable terms, Briouze had not paid off any of his debt, and ignored every deadline. In the end, in order to recover his money, John had been forced to foreclose. In the king's account, the decision to order the sheriff of Gloucester into Briouze's lands in south Wales is presented as a case of sending in the bailiffs to seize goods to the value. Similarly, when William afterwards surrendered castles and hostages, these were simply guarantees that he would in future keep up with his repayments.[21]

There is nothing in John's statement that is actually untrue. Briouze had entered into a large debt for Limerick and not made any attempt to pay it off. But this was not particularly unusual. Money promised for privileges or permissions was almost never paid up front. Men who offered hundreds or even thousands of pounds to have a certain piece of land, or to be sheriff of a particular county; women who offered similar sums for the wardship of their children, or for the right to marry where they chose – all expected to pay off these debts over a number of years. Moreover, some individuals, if they were sufficiently close to the king, or sufficiently powerful that he relied on their political support, might expect never to have to pay anything. William de Briouze seems to have been trading on precisely this assumption. After all, Henry II had taken a very relaxed attitude towards the debts of his magnates, and so too had Richard I.[22]

It was during John's reign that the time-honoured assumption that great men need not worry unduly about their debts to the Crown was disproved. A first sign of change came in 1201 with an amendment to the law, which allowed the king to seize land from a debtor if the land was connected to their debt. It was not until 1207, however, that we start to see this more aggressive attitude being applied in practice. The king's chief financial office, in existence since at least the time of Henry I, was the Exchequer – its name derived from the large chequered cloth, laid out on a table, upon which debts were computed using counters, rather like an abacus. It was here that royal officials and Crown debtors would come to render their accounts, subject to the searching examination of the so-called 'barons of the Exchequer'. From 1207 we can detect a new degree of rigour in the way these men treated magnate debts. Previously, for example, it had been hard for the Exchequer to be sure precisely how much a magnate owed, because debts were enrolled on a county-by-county basis, and great men invariably had estates scattered all over the country. From 1207, however, it became increasingly common for Exchequer officials to group all the debts of a particular magnate together, so that the extent of his liability could be seen in an instant. Roger de Montbegon, the northern baron who had fallen under suspicion in 1204 and surrendered hostages to the king in 1205, was among the first to have his debts treated in this way.[23]

Others actually had their debts called in. Thomas de Moulton had become sheriff of Lincoln in 1205 after promising to give the king 500 marks and five palfreys. But by the spring of 1208 he had fallen behind with his payments, and the Exchequer decided to come down hard on him. Deprived of office in May, he was later arrested on the king's orders and imprisoned in Rochester Castle, 'so that he may not leave until he has paid us everything he owes us, to the last penny'.[24] A similar unremitting attitude was in evidence during the summer of 1208 when John visited northern England. The bishop of Durham had died earlier in the year, and the king had apparently travelled north to ensure that the confiscated episcopal estates were being administered efficiently. This may explain why on leaving Durham he travelled west into Cumbria for an interview with Robert de Vieuxpont. Like William de Briouze, Vieuxpont was a dependable henchman who had served John loyally in Normandy down to his departure in 1203 and who had been richly rewarded as a result, receiving a barony in Cumbria, where he was investing considerable sums in rebuilding castles at Brougham and Brough. He had also been given wide-ranging responsibilities in the north, serving as sheriff of both Derby and Nottingham, and acting as custodian of the confiscated bishoprics of York and Durham. At some point in 1208, however, probably during the king's visit, he lost John's favour; later in the year, he was able to regain it by promising to pay 4,000 marks and surrendering a nephew as a hostage. As with both Briouze and Moulton, the official cause of the king's displeasure was debt: Vieuxpont and his deputies had apparently not paid as much into the Exchequer as had been expected. But it is tempting to suspect that, as with Briouze, there were other reasons. Vieuxpont had been keeper of Rouen Castle at the time of Arthur's disappearance.[25]

The essential point is that the workings of the Exchequer were far from being impartial or impersonal. In his self-defensive letter of 1210 John declared that Briouze's possessions had been seized 'according to the custom of England and the law of the Exchequer', as if to imply that these were automatic processes, the law following its due course. In fact the opposite was true: the law of the Exchequer, like the law of the Forest, was highly whimsical. The barons of the Exchequer might follow certain routines and procedures, and would always endeavour to maximize the Crown's revenue. But it was the king who ultimately controlled the collection of debt. He could tell the Exchequer to relax its demands or distrain an individual with particular harshness; he could choose to cancel a debt entirely or call it all in at once; he could require fines that were token or extortionate, and set repayment terms that were lenient or punitive. John had not only changed the law on debt to make the property of debtors vulnerable as never before; he had also decided from 1207–8 to enforce it ruthlessly, using fiscal measures as a way of exerting political control.[26]

In order to administer such control, the king required the right sort of personnel. If there was one person apart from John himself who was supplying the new and exacting tone in royal government, it was Peter des Roches. Peter was a native of Anjou (or, more specifically, the Touraine), a scion of the same knightly dynasty that had produced William des Roches. But whereas William had ultimately abandoned John because of his treatment of Arthur, Peter had remained in the king's service to become his most indispensable counsellor. Trained as a clerk in his youth, he had also picked up other useful skills along the way; according to Roger of Wendover he was more practised at besieging castles than preaching the word of God. Nonetheless, royal favour marked him out for ecclesiastical preferment, and in 1204 John nominated him as the new bishop of Winchester (in the face of opposition from some of the local clergy, which delayed his enthronement until 1206). From this point on he was clearly associated with the king's financial policies. 'The warrior of Winchester, up at the Exchequer / Keen on finance, slack at scripture', ran a contemporary satirical poem. It was, however, another financial institution, the Chamber, that des Roches made his own. The Chamber was the department of the royal household responsible for the king's personal finances. Unlike the Exchequer, which sat permanently at Westminster, it travelled with the king wherever he went, paying for his immediate needs, whether domestic (food, wine, clothes) or military (crossbows, mercenaries, siege engines). One of des Roches' innovations, carried through in the summer of 1207, had been to create new regional treasuries in castles such as Bristol, Corfe, Marlborough and Nottingham, where money could be stored and collected by the Chamber, bypassing the slower, more cumbersome processes of the Exchequer. It was the kind of hand-to-mouth, quasi-military system he had operated for the king on the Continent until the collapse of 1204.[27]

To run such a system required a more traditional type of sheriff. The earlier experiment of having 'custodian' sheriffs, carefully accounting for every penny of profit at the Exchequer, was largely abandoned during the financial year 1207–8. Instead, John began to appoint tough enforcers, allowing them once again to keep the profits of their office, provided they also kept order. Several of these men had previously served as military captains on the Continent. Hubert de Burgh, who had reportedly ignored the king's order to blind Arthur in 1202, had nevertheless been appointed as keeper of Chinon Castle, and had been captured in 1205 when the fortress finally fell to Philip Augustus. In 1207 John eventually got round to paying his ransom and the following year Hubert replaced Thomas de Moulton as sheriff of Lincoln. Another military captain and mercenary leader, Gerard d'Athée, had been commander of the garrison at Loches until that castle was taken in 1205. John brought him to England in the autumn of 1207 and appointed him as sheriff of Gloucester at the start of the following year, in which capacity he led the attacks on

William de Briouze. After Briouze's submission Athée was also appointed as sheriff of Hereford, making him the most powerful individual in the Welsh March. He took his name from Athée-sur-Cher, just outside Tours, and had close connections with that other man from the same region, Peter des Roches. A number of men, with the same connections of family and neighbourhood, followed in their wake. Later in 1208, one of Athée's relatives, Philip Marc, became sheriff of Nottingham and Derby, replacing Robert de Vieuxpont.[28]

If John was cracking down on debt as a way of exerting political control, it was still the case that he needed vast sums of money. The two-year truce he had agreed with Philip Augustus in 1206 was set to expire on 13 October, and John fully intended to be back in France to resume the military struggle. No sooner had he abandoned his plan to sail to Ireland in March 1208 than he was issuing new orders, instructing the men of all maritime districts to have their ships ready to sail from Portsmouth on 1 June. As before, any vessels that were not provided voluntarily were to be seized, and dire consequences were threatened for those who disobeyed. But despite these threats, the results were evidently disappointing, for when the king arrived in Portsmouth at the end of May no departure took place. It was probably at this stage, angry at the inadequacy of preparation, that he ordered severe reprisals against the men of the Cinque Ports. Gervase of Canterbury, well placed to know, describes how the king 'hanged some of them, and put others to the sword, imprisoned many, bound them in irons, and eventually released them only in return for pledges and money'. This last part, at least, can be verified, for the Cinque Ports did indeed make a fine of 1,000 marks for the king's goodwill. Fresh orders were given for a new muster in September, and throughout the summer, while John took himself off to northern England, his officials strained every sinew to find him the necessary fleet and crews. But, once again, his plans went awry. On 16 September, just five days before the muster date, the king suddenly ordered some of the ships at Portsmouth to redeploy.[29]

The reason was a fresh rebellion by William de Briouze. According to John's later propaganda letter – our only source – Briouze and two of his sons, William and Reginald, had gathered a large force of men and tried to retake Radnor, Brecon and Hay, the three castles he had surrendered to the king in April. Their attack was apparently well timed – the constables had gone to collect their salaries from their commander, Gerard d'Athée – but nevertheless unsuccessful. Having failed to take the castles they went on to attack the royal garrison in nearby Leominster, killing some of the crossbowmen and sergeants, wounding many others, and burning half the town to the ground.

Briouze's rebellion was a total failure. As soon as Gerard d'Athée heard the news he launched an immediate and overwhelming counteroffensive; within days Briouze's men were deserting him and pledging their allegiance to the king. Briouze himself was soon a fugitive, 'retreating from one place to the next', and by the end of September, barely a fortnight after his abortive attempt to recover his castles, he had run out of places to hide. Gathering up his wife, sons and his few remaining followers, he fled to Ireland.[30]

Briouze's short-lived revolt did not by itself unduly disrupt John's plans for France. When the news had broken he had ordered most of the ships to remain in Portsmouth and await his arrival. The unsuccessful rebellion did, however, set off a chain reaction of events elsewhere in Wales that would have far greater consequences. As soon as Briouze had revolted, John had given his lands in Brecon to another of his intimate counsellors, Peter fitz Herbert. Fitz Herbert had barely had time to take possession of his prize, however, before these lands came under attack from the Welsh.[31]

Beyond the marcher lordships that lay along its southern and eastern edges, Wales was still an independent, Celtic country. Like Ireland it had no single ruler, but a galaxy of petty kings and princes, all competing with one another as well as their Anglo-Norman neighbours. One of these princes, Gwenwynwyn of Powys, had long been a rival of William de Briouze, and saw in his opponent's fall the opportunity to expand his power. As soon as Briouze faltered, Gwenwynwyn moved into his lordship of Brecon, where he immediately came to blows with the new owner, Peter fitz Herbert.

It was this fresh contest in the March that caused John to abandon his plans for the Continent. On 29 September he gave permission to all his knights and bachelors to assist fitz Herbert in defending his lands. A day or so later he decided to follow in their wake, moving rapidly from Dorset towards the Welsh border. Confronted with a furious John and the forces he had been planning to lead into France, Gwenwynwyn quickly submitted, and appeared before the king at Shrewsbury on 8 October. The terms he received were terrible. In return for the king sparing his life and limbs, the prince was required to find twenty hostages, and obliged to remain in royal custody until all of them had been handed over. The hostages only bought Gwenwynwyn his liberty; all of his lands were confiscated.[32]

His expedition to France now dead in the water, John left the Welsh border and travelled along the Thames towards Westminster, arriving there in the last week of October. But during the rest of the autumn the fallout from the Briouze revolt continued. Just as the eclipse of Briouze had enticed Gwenwynwyn, so too the fall of Gwenwynwyn had created an irresistible temptation for his neighbour. Llywelyn, the prince of the northern region of Gwynedd, was easily the most successful of all the native rulers of Wales, thanks to a winning combination of military ability, pragmatism and luck. Having established his right to rule Gwynedd in the 1190s by fighting off rivals within his own family, he cemented his position by striking up a good relation-ship with John. At the start of his reign John had recognized Llywelyn's rights and taken him into his protection, and in 1205 the prince had been married to the king's illegitimate daughter, Joan. This was a singular honour for a Welsh ruler, and it had clearly marked Llywelyn out as John's favourite.[33]

But when, towards the end of 1208, the prince invaded Powys, lately vacated by Gwenwynwyn, he soon discovered that his father-in-law's favour had its limits. At first John seemed to take an indulgent line. On Christmas Day he sent a letter to Llywelyn, assuring him that he had forgiven the prince his recent trespasses, and continued to regard him with fatherly affection. One month later, however, the king was back at Shrewsbury, at the head of a large army, poised to invade Llywelyn's lands. Whether the prince had committed some new offence in the meantime, or whether John had simply been dissimulating at Christmas, is unclear. But Llywelyn, like Gwenwynwyn, rapidly submitted. The terms he received are unknown, but were clearly far better than imposed on his rival the previous October. Llywelyn was left at liberty, and in possession of all his lands, including his recent conquests.[34]

Thus, by the end of January 1209, Wales was finally settled, bringing to an end a turbulent five months. The king's plan to return to the Continent had been wrecked, but by the start of the new year it was apparent that his overseas subjects were coping in spite of his absence. When the truce with France had expired in October, Philip Augustus had launched an attack on John's ally, the viscount of Thouars, but soon into the campaign the French king had fallen ill and been forced to retire to Paris. Although his deputies continued the fighting, they made no substantial gains and the territorial status quo held. Philip was in any case distracted by problems elsewhere in France: a rebellion in Auvergne, and, in the Languedoc, the murder of a papal legate by Cathar heretics. The latter had led to pressure from the pope, who wanted him to crush the heretics by leading a crusade.[35]

By the start of 1209 it was the pope, rather than the king of France, who seemed to pose the greater threat to John's security. Innocent's reaction to the seizure of Church property carried out the previous year had been surprisingly muted. He was convinced that the interdict would soon persuade John to change his mind about the archbishop of Canterbury, and encouraged by the exchange of messengers that had continued throughout the summer. These negotiations, however, had petered out in the autumn, and by the new year the pope had realized that his strategy was not going to work: his adversary was quite content to let matters rest, and in the meantime enjoy the massive contribution that the Church's confiscated property was making to his revenues. On 12 January he dispatched an uncompromising letter to John, threatening him with excommunication. The king would be 'accursed and cut off from the community of the faithful' if he did not agree to the terms proposed the previous year. Innocent informed John that he had three months to comply, and made it clear that this was his final warning. 'Look, the bow is at full stretch', he wrote. 'Beloved son, avoid the arrow which turns not back!'[36]

The king had to take this escalation seriously. As we've seen, even before the interdict had been imposed, Innocent had written to the nobles of England, urging them to set aside their loyalty to John until he made peace with the Church. The king might have taken that less seriously had he not in the meantime had his plans disrupted by the rebellion of one of his greatest subjects – a man who was still at large in Ireland. How much easier it would be for others to justify such rebellion were he to be excommunicated. Moreover, the pope was already trying to persuade Philip Augustus to crush the Church's enemies in southern France by launching a crusade against them. If he suddenly licensed a similar attack on England, Philip, who had already planned to invade England in 1205, might need little persuading. Such considerations meant that Innocent's letter had to be answered, and John had to be seen to act. Accordingly, just before Easter, he reopened negotiations, and issued letters of safe conduct for Master Simon Langton, brother of the unwanted archbishop.[37]

A few days later, the king's attention was suddenly focused elsewhere. On 10 April he wrote to William the Lion, the king of Scots, asking for a meeting. This was somewhat unusual, because for many years John had shown little interest in attending to the concerns of his northern neighbour. Having obtained William's homage, very publicly, at Lincoln in 1200, John had repeatedly postponed or ignored the Scottish king's plea to hear his claim to Northumbria. In the intervening eight years they had met only twice, with inconclusive results.

In the spring of 1209, by contrast, John went out of his way to meet William. Previously the onus had been on the Scottish king to come south, for meetings at York, Lincoln or even Northampton. But when John wrote on 10 April he was already about to enter Yorkshire, and proposing to come as far north as Newcastle. The tone of his letter was friendly and accommodating. He rejoiced that William (who was in his mid-sixties) had recovered from his recent illness, and expressed a desire to conclude their long-running dispute. No wonder the Scottish king, in spite of his infirmities, responded eagerly. The two kings met at Newcastle a fortnight later, with unknown but apparently amicable results, and evidently some sort of settlement plan. William returned to Scotland and summoned a council of his leading subjects to approve it. They met on 24 May at Stirling, and dispatched a high-ranking embassy into England with their reply.

But when these ambassadors reached John's court they found him in a very different mood, thundering threats against the king of Scots and Scotland in general. What had changed? The answer seems to be that since their meeting in April John had discovered that William had allied, or attempted to ally, with Philip Augustus, just as he had tried to do at the start of John's reign. It seems very likely that John had suspected this was the case all along, and that his sudden desire to meet with William after Easter had in fact been an attempt to sniff out the conspiracy. If so, his suspicions had clearly been confirmed in the month that followed: the moment of truth may have come on 28 May, when the king, then at Arundel Castle in Sussex, paid half a mark to 'Fulcher, a secret messenger who came from overseas'.

The substance of the allegation is given further proof by John's reaction. According to Gervase of Canterbury, he demanded that William should surrender either his son, Alexander, or three castles on the Scottish border. When William refused, John threatened war, and summoned an army to invade. In the last week of July he marched north from Nottingham, leading what one contemporary called 'an innumerable army'. The Scottish king, who had been sending messages to play for time, assembled a force to resist the invasion at Roxburgh, but once again fell ill. When John drew up his host on the border at Norham at the start of August, William immediately submitted. He was forced to accept a humiliating peace, the outstanding feature of which was that it required him to hand over his two eldest daughters, Margaret and Isabella, to John's custody. Both girls were in their mid-teens and unmarried. John announced that he would marry Margaret to his own son, Henry, and find Isabella a husband of appropriate status from among the English nobility. The point was clearly for John to control the marriages, from which we can reasonably conclude that the plot he had uncovered involved one or other of the girls marrying Philip Augustus. As an additional security measure, William was obliged to hand over a further thirteen hostages, and promised to pay 15,000 marks within the next two years. This peace was imposed, according to one chronicler, 'against the will of the Scots'.[38]

Scotland may have been solved, but the problem of the pope remained. The talks proposed in March had come to nothing, but on 13 July, just days before setting out against the Scots, John had suddenly become earnest about reaching a settlement. He cannot have known by this date that, three weeks earlier, Innocent had authorized his excommunication at Stephen Langton's discretion. There may therefore be some truth in the comment of Gervase of Canterbury, who claims that the king's resumption of negotiations had been caused by murmurings in the ranks of his army about the perils of marching into battle against the Scots while England was under interdict. As everyone knew, it was God who determined the outcome of battles.[39]

Even as John was browbeating William the Lion into submission at Norham, therefore, his leading ministers were meeting with the pope's representatives at Dover, trying to hammer out an acceptable agreement. By 9 August they had drafted a set of terms. Stephen Langton was to be admitted to England and installed as archbishop of Canterbury; the monks of Canterbury, driven into exile in 1207, were to be allowed to return; and the Church as a whole was to be compensated for its financial losses, with the money paid by the end of the month.[40]

Once the Scottish king had submitted, however, and with no dissenting soldiery in need of appeasement, John's enthusiasm for a settlement started to wane. When these terms were brought to him on his journey south from Scotland, he found them unsatisfactory, and immediately began to stall. On 23 August he wrote to the envoys at Dover, inviting them to come to Northampton for further talks. But the envoys doubted the value of his safe conducts, and feared they would be seized if they ventured inland. On 2 September they issued their ultimatum. The king must accept the terms as drafted by 23 September, or face excommunication a fortnight later.[41]

John's response was to take countermeasures of a kind never before witnessed in England. Although he no longer faced the pressing problem of desertion, his fear remained that if he was excommunicated Innocent might absolve his subjects from their loyalty, or even seek to sponsor an invasion. When he heard that the Church's sentence was imminent, he left the Midlands and went directly to Marlborough, his chief castle in southern England. From there on 13 September he wrote to Stephen Langton himself, inviting him to come to Dover for a personal interview. But this was merely a tactic to buy time for his actual response.

On the same day, dozens of other letters were dispatched to every sheriff in England, from Kent to Cumbria, advising them of his intention of taking a new general oath of loyalty. John had, of course, exacted such an oath before, in 1205, when he had been worried about a French invasion and internal dissension. When these anxieties returned to haunt him in 1209, however, he conceived of something bigger and altogether more powerful: a mass assembly, where his subjects would pledge their allegiance to him in person, against the backdrop of one of his most impressive castles. At the end of September, according to Gervase of Canterbury, 'all the men in England, rich and poor and middling, aged fifteen and upwards, came together at Marlborough on the king's orders, and there they swore fealty, both to the king and to his son, Henry'. The comments of other chroniclers indicate that John's summons actually applied only to freemen, and that some of them were permitted to take their oaths locally. But if Gervase was guilty of exaggerating, it was with good reason. Other evidence makes it clear that freemen came to Marlborough in vast numbers: thousands, and perhaps tens of thousands. The king seems to have required in particular the presence of townsmen, especially the men of London, almost all of whom are said to have attended. Later entries on the Exchequer rolls show that draconian fines were imposed for those who failed to do so.[42]

The reason for insisting on this mass migration was John's desire to forge a stronger bond with his subjects. Although Gervase speaks only of fealty – i.e. a promise of fidelity – other writers make it clear that the king additionally required those who came to Marlborough to do homage – to kneel down before him and declare that they were his men, regardless of the fact that they might not hold their lands from him (which was what an act of homage ordinarily implied). This, along with the pledge of allegiance to John's two-year-old son and heir, and the uniquely massive scale of the gathering, made the Oath of Marlborough an unprecedented event, and one which would never be repeated. It was a ceremonial, charismatic rejoinder to the spiritual authority of the pope; a reminder of the awesome, mystical power of the monarchy.[43]

A few days after this extraordinary spectacle, Stephen Langton arrived at Dover, as invited. The king, informed of his arrival, travelled to Kent, and stopped at Chilham Castle, not far from Canterbury, from where the two sides could easily communicate. But although they came physically close, no meeting took place. Gervase opined that John's mind had been changed by 'the tongues of evil detractors', but the truth was that on both sides, minds were already made up, and wedded to irreconcilable positions. The king wanted a guarantee of his rights and dignity, the pope required unconditional surrender. Having just taken elaborate steps to buttress his power, John saw no reason to compromise. He turned and left for London, leaving Langton to sail back to France, with inevitable consequences. One month later, the king was excommunicated.[44]

John successfully prevented an official proclamation of the sentence in England, but the news inevitably found its way across the Channel. It quickly became common knowledge – the subject, according to Roger of Wendover, of secret conversation everywhere. And yet, although it compounded the king's notoriety, the consequences of being cursed by the Church were far less disastrous than he had feared. There was no rebellion and no foreign invasion; the pope did not declare him deposed. The only immediate effect of his excommunication was the removal of the remaining members of the episcopate. In the final weeks of the year, the bishops of Bath, Lincoln, Rochester and Salisbury left the country, joining their colleagues from Worcester, Ely and London who had left at the start of the interdict. By Christmas, the only remaining bishop in England was 'the warrior of Winchester', Peter des Roches, singularly unperturbed by his master's pariah status. For John, of course, the departure of the other prelates had one very positive consequence, as their confiscated estates further swelled his revenues.[45]

To his critics John seemed all powerful, invulnerable. 'There was no one in the land who could resist his will in anything', said Gervase of Canterbury, commenting on the flight of the bishops. 'The king himself was the only power in the land, and feared neither God nor men.' Roger of Wendover, with more bitterness, observed that the laity seemed unperturbed by John's excommunication. When he celebrated Christmas at Windsor a few weeks later, 'all the nobles of England were present and conversing with him, notwithstanding the sentence under which he was bound'.[46]

But neither chronicler was entirely correct. There were several men who were *not* present at John's court that Christmas – men he had good reason to fear. One was William Marshal, who was in Ireland, having returned there soon after his reconciliation with the king in 1208, though not before being required to hand over one of his sons as a hostage.[47] Another was Walter de Lacy, who had also returned to Ireland, to join his brother Hugh, the earl of Ulster, who had never left. And, of course, there was William de Briouze, the cause of so much disruption during 1208, down but not out. He too was in Ireland, having fled there after his abortive rebellion that autumn.

In the aftermath of Briouze's revolt, the king had spent much time and energy imposing his will on England, Scotland and Wales. The king of Scots had surrendered his daughters to stave off invasion, and his son, Alexander, had done homage to John soon afterwards. The princes of Wales – those who had not been broken – had come to do homage to him en masse at Woodstock in mid-October 1209, just as men from all over England had done at Marlborough a fortnight earlier. In every part of mainland Britain, people had been forcefully and dramatically reminded of the extent of the king of England's power. Only in Ireland did men continue to resist him, convinced that they were beyond his reach.[48]

John had tried the soft approach. In the winter of 1208–9, not long after Briouze's flight, he had appointed a new justiciar of Ireland, replacing the discredited Meiler fitz Henry with John de Gray, the dependable bishop of Norwich (for whom it was a convenient posting, since the interdict did not extend across the Irish Sea). Gray had tried to apprehend Briouze, but discovered the fugitive and his family were being sheltered by their friends and relatives, first by William Marshal, later by Walter and Hugh de Lacy. Against these powerful magnates, the authority of the justiciar was no match, and they rejected his demands to hand over Briouze. The king himself, according to his own account, sent messages to them, reminding them of their fealty, and telling them they ought not to be harbouring his enemies. All he received was a procrastinating reply, saying that they would cease to shelter Briouze if he did not make amends by a certain date. The deadline came and went, but the promise was not kept.[49]

This was, it seems, more than just passive resistance. The Lacy brothers, at least, were actively plotting to bring John down. A letter survives from Philip Augustus, addressed to one of the brothers, referring to the war they were planning to wage against their king with the help of friends in both England and Ireland. It is unclear whether this plot was linked to the secret negotiations between Philip and the king of Scots that John discovered in the spring of 1209. It is also unclear whether or not John himself ever became aware of it. What is certain is that by the end of the year he had lost patience with his defiant Irish magnates and decided to deal with them in person. 'We could not tolerate their many outrages,' he explained in his letter, 'and assembled an army to go into Ireland.'[50]

Financial preparations for the campaign were already under way by the start of the new year. John had demanded another scutage in 1209 – the eighth of his reign – and by 1210 was busy calling it in, imposing exceptionally heavy fines on those who chose not to supply him with military service, and seizing the lands of those who could not pay. He also imposed an arbitrary tax, known as tallage, on all towns and royal manors, as well as the confiscated estates of the Church, again with exceptional results: Bristol and Colchester, for example, each paid 1,000 marks. During the first four months of the year the king tore around the country at his usual frantic pace, moving from Dorset to Durham and back in his quest for more cash. Another new regional treasury, operational by early February, was created at Northampton to collect it all, and in April its contents were transferred to Bristol. John arrived there in the middle of May, before proceeding through south Wales to reach the coast of Pembrokeshire at the end of the month, anxious to see what his millions of silver pennies had achieved.[51]

For once he was not disappointed. All the evidence suggests that the force that had been mustered near Haverford was massive. A surviving payroll reveals that there were more than 1,000 sergeants and crossbowmen, as well as 800 mounted knights. And these were merely the men who had agreed to serve for wages.

A great many more must have turned out to fulfil their customary military service to the king, swelling his army to many thousands. In anticipation of siege warfare, he had recruited miners, masons, ditchers and carpenters. Hundreds of tonnes of food and drink had been stockpiled to feed them, and hundreds more tonnes of grain to feed their horses. The total scale of the operation is perhaps best conveyed by the fact that John had 700 ships: a fleet equivalent in size to the one used by William the Conqueror to invade England in 1066.[52]

News of this inexorable military build-up found its way to Ireland and caused certain people to reconsider their positions. At some point in the spring William Marshal (whose first loyalty was always to himself) crossed to England and made his peace with the king, agreeing to join the expedition when it sailed. William de Briouze also sought safe conduct to come and treat for peace, but (according to John's account) once it was granted he went to Herefordshire and again tried to raise a revolt. When the king was on 'the shore of the Irish Sea at Pembroke', Briouze sought licence to negotiate for a second time, and drew near enough to communicate via intermediaries. He apparently offered the gargantuan sum of 40,000 marks to regain John's goodwill, to which the king replied that he 'knew well that this was beyond his capacity, but more within that of his wife'. John suggested that William should join his imminent expedition so they could discuss the matter with Matilda and reach an agreement. William, who clearly had a more realistic understanding about what John's coming to Ireland would entail, declined the invitation and withdrew to his refuge in Wales.[53]

The great armada sailed from Haverford on 19 June 1210 and landed near Waterford the following morning, just as its smaller predecessor had done when John had crossed to Ireland twenty-five years earlier. The king was immediately joined by his justiciar, John de Gray, leading a force of Irish friendlies, and other Irish lords who appeared to offer their submission. The royal army advanced through the Marshal lordship of Leinster, stopping at the Marshal's castle in Kilkenny, and arriving in Dublin by the end of the first week. There, on 28 June, messengers arrived from Walter de Lacy, offering their lord's submission and seeking to blame the situation on his brother, Hugh. John responded by banishing Walter, who may have left the country at that moment, and advancing into his lordship of Meath, seizing all his castles (including the mighty donjon at Trim) for the Crown, and confiscating all his lands, some of which were granted out to the king's followers.[54]

The remaining target was Hugh de Lacy, who was sheltering Matilda de Briouze and her family. When he realized that John was moving northwards into his territory, Hugh burnt some of his castles and retreated. The king pursued him, taking other castles with ease as their garrisons gave up without a fight. Eventually John arrived at Carrickfergus, the greatest and most impressive of all the Lacy strongholds, where the earl's diehard supporters had holed up in the hope of making a stand. The castle fell after a short siege and all inside were taken prisoner, but neither Hugh nor Matilda were among them. They had fled across the sea, first to the Isle of Man, where they were pursued by John's forces, and then quickly on to Galloway in south-west Scotland. The earl managed to evade capture, along with Briouze's son Reginald, and eventually made his way to France, where he was reunited with his exiled brother Walter.

But the rest of the fugitives were not so lucky. Matilda and her daughter Annora, together with William de Briouze the younger and his wife and children, were all arrested by Duncan of Carrick, a local Scottish lord, descended from a bastard line of Henry I and later richly rewarded for his service with lands in Ireland. His delighted second cousin dispatched two ships and a force of crossbowmen and sergeants to escort them back to Carrickfergus.[55]

Having driven the Lacy brothers into exile and captured most of the family of William de Briouze, John's main objectives in coming to Ireland had been achieved. He returned south to Dublin, taking more castles and receiving more submissions as he went, arriving in the capital on 18 August. One week later, and barely two months after his arrival, he sailed back across the Irish Sea to Wales.[56]

With him sailed his unfortunate captives, Matilda de Briouze and her family, who were taken to Bristol Castle and imprisoned. According to the Anonymous of Béthune, a very well-informed source for these events, Matilda was a formidable woman, well liked by everyone, who was not only beautiful but also valiant, vigorous and wise. As the wife of a marcher lord she had kept up the war against the Welsh and conquered much from them. On one occasion she had boasted to the count of Aumale that she owned more than 12,000 cows. In her negotiations with John, however, she seems to have veered between defiance and despair. According to the king's own account, she had initially offered him 40,000 marks to spare the lives of her husband, her family and herself, only to change her mind three days later. But by the time they were back in England she had changed her mind again, and upped her offer by 10,000 marks, agreeing that this extra amount would be paid immediately, and accepting that she and her family would remain in prison until the whole debt of 50,000 marks had been cleared. Having sealed this diabolical pact with the king, she sought permission to speak with her husband.

William de Briouze came in. While John had been in Ireland he had attempted to raise a revolt for the third time, but with pitifully feeble results. With his wife, son and grandchildren now held captive, he agreed to pay the fine as agreed, and was allowed to leave the court in order to begin raising the money. This was, of course, an utterly impossible task – 50,000 marks was a figure equivalent to John's ordinary annual revenue from the whole kingdom. After a while William managed to give his escort the slip and fled across the Channel to France.

When the king sent several leading magnates to tell Matilda what had happened, her old defiance returned. She replied curtly that she would pay nothing of the fine, since all she had left was twenty-four marks of silver, twenty-four gold coins and fifteen ounces of gold. 'So neither then nor afterwards did she, her husband, or anyone else on their behalf, pay me anything of the debt', said John, concluding his lengthy account of the whole sorry saga, hopeful that his subjects would share his indignation, and adding that he had ordered William de Briouze to be outlawed in every shire, 'according to the laws and custom of England'.

What he did not mention was the fate of William's indomitable wife. Matilda, along with her eldest son, William, was removed from Bristol and taken to another royal castle – some chroniclers say Windsor, others Corfe. All agree that once they were there, the two of them were starved to death. According to the Anonymous of Béthune:

On the eleventh day the mother was found dead between her son's legs, still upright but leaning back against her son's chest as a dead woman. The son, who was also dead, sat upright, leaning against the wall as a dead man. So desperate was the mother that she had eaten her son's cheeks. When William de Briouze, who was in Paris, heard this news, he died soon afterwards, many asserting that it was through grief.[57]

Château Gaillard and the Isle of Andely as they appear today, and as they might have appeared during the siege of 1203–4.

The tomb effigies of Henry II and Eleanor of Aquitaine at Fontevraud.